THE MUSLIM ECONOMIC TRAP

THE MUSLIM ECONOMIC TRAP

The Correlation of Government Economic Power
with Present-Day Terrorism

Carol M. Fuller

ISBN 13: 978-1-59298-217-2
ISBN 10: 1-59298-217-4
Library of Congress Catalog Number: 2007943056

Book design and typesetting: Jill Blumer
Printed in the United States of America
First Printing: 2008

12   11   10   09   08   5   4   3   2   1

Beaver's Pond Press

7104 Ohms Lane, Suite 216
Edina, Minnesota 55439 USA
(952) 829-8818
www.BeaversPondPress.com

To order, visit www.BookHouseFulfillment.com or call 1-800-901-3480.
Reseller and special sales discounts available.

CONTENTS

CONTENTS *(Continued)*

INTRODUCTION

In the metropolitan area where I live, a Christian-Muslim Dialogue group has been meeting for about 25 years. I have attended occasionally and have been impressed with the intelligence and sincerity of its participants as we learned about each other's faith and customs. These meetings are a peaceful world apart, however, from the attacks on America by al Qaeda on September 11, 2001.

Like many Americans I was confused and angry, and I wanted to understand. Scholars and journalists told us that one of the causes of this tragedy lies in the high unemployment rates and weak economies in many Muslim countries. Economic stresses drive some young men, those who are especially susceptible to religious fervor, to embrace terror. On the other hand we are told the cause of terrorism is an unfathomable black hatred of everything Western boiling up among religious fundamentalists who are striving for a role in the councils of their governments but have been squelched by autocratic regimes. At times these regimes have been, or are, supported by Western nations in the name of preserving stability. I concluded that the road to some degree of understanding of the suicidal violence of al Qaeda and a small number of other groups was through the economic history and current economic situation of the Middle East.

I was unable, however, to find books that concentrate on economic history in Islam and had to be satisfied with my own compilation of details related to economics and economic conditions. I found this information here and there in many scholarly works and articles on the history of Islam. The notes I took grew into the economic history presented in the **Historical Background** of my book.

In comparing the Muslim world, its history and its present condition, with the world I know, Europe and America, I was struck by the difference in ownership of productive property, particularly land. (Until very modern times the dominant economy everywhere was agrarian, and nearly all production was from the land.) In Europe private property was the lever of economic strength used by individuals to wrest liberties from the king, at least from the English king, something many of us learned in school. In contrast, private ownership of productive property is almost totally lacking in Russian history, and has never been vigorous in Muslim lands.

Private ownership of productive property has been handicapped in Muslim lands by the requirements of their religion and by customs inherited from oriental civilizations. This situation acts against economic development and weighs heavily against the formation of a stable, empowered middle class. Instead, beliefs and customs promote a steady flow of ownership of productive property to the government and a generous but lesser flow to the clerics—but always away from ordinary people. Other customs depress the economy: education oriented to religious fundamentalism, failure to utilize the talents of women, and intolerance. A discussion of these matters is in **Part One** of the book.

For present-day economic conditions I made great use of the figures and estimates in the *Index of Economic Freedom* published by the Heritage Foundation and the *Wall Street Journal* (2002 to 2005). My focus in assembling this information was on countries of the Middle East and North Africa.

When I looked at economic evaluations of certain present-day Muslim countries, I could see a correlation between incidents of terror and overwhelming economic power resting in the hands of governments. The governments that have sponsored or assisted terrorism have ownership or control of high percentages of their countries' productive property. With little or no dependence on taxation they need not listen to the voices of their citizens. These facts and estimates are given in **Part Two** of the book. (For this focus I wish another book had come to my attention earlier: *Where is the Wealth of Nations?* by a team of people at the World Bank, which published the book in 2006.*)

An important book called *The Road to Serfdom* by Friedrich Hayek, the Austrian economist, was published in the midst of World War II. At a time when socialism and central planning by governments were in the ascendancy, he clearly saw the connection between economic control by governments and totalitarianism represented by German Nazism, Italian fascism, and Soviet Communism. In his long academic life he warned against the economic grasp of totalitarianism and argued for free markets and individual choices. In 1974 he received the Nobel Prize in Economics. What an important insight he gave us! Private ownership limits the power of the state and enables democratic institutions to evolve—that is, if other conditions do not interfere, such as intrusions from outside the borders of the state or aggressive wars led by its own leaders, and if out-of-control population growth does not leave multitudes of people without hope.

In finding property ownership to be a key to the turbulence of the Middle East I am not attempting to excuse interference by

---

* Through complex analyses, World Bank authors conclude that an extremely important part of the wealth of each nation is in its "human capital and the quality of formal and informal institutions." The share of this intangible capital rises with the rise in income of nations. "The latter point makes perfect sense—rich countries are rich because of the skills of their populations and the quality of the institutions supporting economic activity." Unfortunately, there is a strong tendency for nations rich in natural resources such as oil to allow their total capital—created, natural and intangible—to deteriorate and to fail to invest in new enterprises and in appropriate education.

Western nations, a bitter complaint of Muslims. The 20th-century struggle against Communism resulted in Western offenses against the Islamic people and elsewhere. Around the world a great many nationalist movements had communist elements, and America in particular felt it had to actively counter them. Hence, the CIA became involved. As seen by William Blum, a journalist who resigned from the State Department in 1967, "From 1945 to 2003 the U.S. attempted to overthrow more than 40 foreign governments, and to crush more than 30 populist-nationalist movements fighting against intolerable regimes."[1]

The struggle of the West against communism brought particularly deplorable outcomes in the Middle East. The Shah of Iran, supported by the CIA in the 1950s against a threatened diminishing of his power, continued to be supported even when a popular uprising unseated him in 1979. This revolution was non-sectarian at first but was preempted by ayatollahs and their followers who set up a new type of government ostensibly democratic but with real power given to religious judges. It wasn't long before Iran created Hezbollah, a corps of terrorists to protect their pattern of government, and then exported Hezbollah to other countries.

Another unfavorable outcome of American action came from involvement in the Afghan war against the Soviet Union in the 1990s: the rise of the Taliban dictatorship and Osama bin Laden as the founder of al Qaeda. Then, too, the United States supported Saddam in the Iraq-Iran war of the 1980s, a dictator irrationally cruel to his own people and so base that in the 1990s he brought unforgivable scandal to the United Nations. He sponsored terrorism in Palestine and encouraged the perception that he was stockpiling atomic weapons, giving reasons for the invasion of Iraq in the spring of 2003.

1. William Bloom, *Killing Hope: U.S. Military and CIA Interventions since World War II*, revised 2003.

These and other untoward U.S. actions give the word "blowback" a special meaning in the American lexicon.

The main theme of this book is this: customs of private property ownership supported by a rule of law either help foster prosperity or smother it. Islamic countries lack these customs and rules, and so lack widespread prosperity and freedom. Western countries, however, were built atop such customs, principles, and rules, and have enjoyed historically unrivalled prosperity and freedom.

A stunning example of the adoption and subsequent benefits of such a social-political-economic framework occurred during General Douglas MacArthur's administration of Japan after World War II. With the acquiescence of the defeated Emperor of Japan, he fundamentally changed the government's treatment of commercial affairs, particularly by establishing individual property rights and a rule of law. The Japanese experience symbolizes a bedrock relationship: private property protected by—and in turn promoting—law, freedom, and prosperity. After a few decades, Japanese producers created world-class industrial efficiency and enviable business acumen, challenging the West with their business.

I am not an expert in history, the Middle East, Islam, global politics, or the like. I am an inquisitive, somewhat analytical, concerned citizen. I sought to learn from recognized scholars and journalists on Islam, on the Middle East, the war on terror, and related affairs. I found scholarly authors who are relatively unknown to the general public as well as respected journalists producing bestsellers, and I followed the newspapers and other media. But I sought to interpret this knowledge in ways that make sense to me.

I believe Muslims should not be offended by an economic emphasis on their history. Islam encompasses all aspects of life, including economic matters, government, law, education, community relations, the family, marriage, daily life, and more. Islam is a "holistic" faith of customs and practices that involve the full range of human activities. Economic matters affect basic survival, but also operate psychologically to affect human pride, ambition, satisfaction, frustration, or despair.

I begin my survey of economic influences in Islam with Muhammad, the man and the Prophet. I then offer a brief, introductory history of Islam before moving on to current beliefs and practices of Muslims that impact their economic situation and relate to Islamic terrorism.

In **Part Three** of the book I return to history, this time to the history of military slavery, modern terrorism, and the relationship between the two. In the final chapter I summarize some of the reforms suggested by Muslim leaders and scholars and point out how such changes might improve the economic condition of ordinary people in the Islamic world.

Carol Fuller

HISTORICAL BACKGROUND: ECONOMIC INFLUENCES ON ISLAM

MUHAMMAD, PROPHET AND MAN OF THIS WORLD

Muhammad was experienced in long-distance trade before revelations led him to become a religious leader. He succeeded in uniting the tribes of the Arabian Peninsula through preaching, sometimes through battle, and often through diplomacy and the taking of daughters of tribal chieftains as his wives. In these efforts many tribesmen in Arabia accepted his belief in Allah and his way of life called Islam.

Today many people picture Muhammad as a charismatic warrior-prophet leading tribesmen out of Arabia into battle against the great empires of that day, subduing all before them as they built their own vast empire. Not so. Such campaigns erupted out of Arabia beginning in 634, nearly two years after his death. So who was Muhammad?

The Early Years, a Period of Tribal Honor and Freedom for Women

Muhammad was born around the year 570 of the current era (C.E.) in Arabia, a land of impoverished feuding tribes and clans. He lived in Mecca, a date-producing oasis in western Arabia located near a sanctuary of many gods.* Arab tribes met there peaceably once a year to trade and worship. The area, far too dry for farming, sat at a crossroads of trade routes. The north-south route ran from Syria in the north to Yemen at the southern tip of the Arabian Peninsula. Ships also sailed from a port near Mecca west across the Red Sea to Africa. From Yemen merchant ships headed east to India. The trade routes attracted raiders from the steppes who preyed upon caravans and also raided villages.

---

*Three hundred-some gods were represented by naturally occurring, oddly-shaped rocks, and one called Allah was especially honored.

Successful raids brought honor to a tribe. The moral ideal of Arabs was bravery in battle (but not needless risk-taking), loyalty, patience in misfortune, persistence in revenge, protection of the weak, defiance of the strong, and generosity to those in need and to strangers. Arabs excelled in poetry, unwritten, and the merits of one's tribe were expressed in poetry. Of course, honor was assured by taking up the sword in reaction to an insult or to harm done to a family or clan member, and some feuds were long-lasting.

In 600, at about age 30, Muhammad, according to tradition, was driving camels for a woman named Khadija, a wealthy merchant. She had inherited her business from two banker husbands, and she actively managed it. She proposed marriage to Muhammad, who accepted. Their marriage was monogamous, producing five children who survived. In pre-Islamic Arab societies women had freedom to run businesses, propose marriage, arrange the marriage contract, dress as they wished, and perhaps to have more than one husband. They could initiate divorce, and wealth could be inherited through female family lines.

Old Values Clashed with the Changing Economy

The economy in and around Mecca had long been that of the nomadic tribe where grazing land was held in common, and stock animals were owned by individuals or families. (Feisty, mean camels needed individual masters.) It was being changed by commerce and banking. "If we are to look for an economic change correlated with the origin of Islam, then it is here that we must look . . . . In the rise of Mecca to wealth and power we have a movement from nomadic to mercantile economy but no readjustment of social, moral, intellectual, and religious attitudes of the community." [2]

2. WILLIAM MONTGOMERY WATT, *Muhammad in Mecca*, Oxford University Press, 77.

Muhammad, an agent in his wife's business, must often have pondered the raiding of caravans as a problem for business and for general prosperity. If all Arabian tribes worshipped one god, might peace come? Could caravans travel in safety? Might prosperity grow? Muhammad knew the importance of trade. The Qur'an, which he recited later, contains verses recognizing the life-giving role of caravans and merchant ships. During the years of his ministry, his actions indicate that the economic welfare of his followers was never far from his mind.

Meccans, still members of an Arabic tribe, felt alienated and distressed when some merchants accumulated wealth and were reluctant to share with others. But, of course, merchants need to have an inventory to trade, and bankers need to accumulate money for lending. Muhammad saw the need for wealth, but was dismayed when many began disregarding old values and were becoming obsessed with accumulating wealth.

One night while meditating he became frightened by a brilliant light and by the information it seemed to impart to him. The message was stark and clear: There is no god but Allah, and Muhammad is his prophet. After days or weeks spent in fear and dread, he began to tell others, beginning with his family. He gathered a following called "the Righteous," and his messages increasingly admonished people to give to orphans—Muhammad was an orphan—and to the poor.

Opposition in Mecca

He preached against an obsession with accumulating wealth. At first his verses were not so laced with dire threats of eternal fires of hell as they were later on. He simply said there is more credit with Allah for charity than for accumulating money. Some people he converted; some became enemies. His message was not immediately popular, but it was immediately threatening to those in power. The prospect of one single god implied economic and political changes. One god, if accepted, would replace the shrines to various gods that were near Mecca and bring an end to the gifts that pilgrims left with Meccan caretakers. At the same time Meccan leaders began to fear Muhammad as a political power. They retaliated with a boycott of his clan and of allied clans. They cut off business with them, prohibited loans to them, and forbade marriage into those clans. After three years under the boycott, the Righteous descended into poverty. Perhaps hardships contributed to the deaths of two people Muhammad relied on, his uncle-and-protector and his wife. Three more years of struggle and failure to gain an economic footing in Mecca followed.

Muslims, the "New Tribe," Bring Peace to Medina

Since Muhammad's followers united members of several clans, he had created what amounted to a "new tribe" in Mecca. People in Medina, a collection of farming villages 200-some miles north of Mecca, observed the internal harmony of Muhammad's new tribe. Leaders from Medina asked Muhammad to serve their community as a judge because Medina had suffered from a very destructive war among their clans. Muhammad's "new tribe," calling themselves the Righteous, had the potential of overcoming differences among clan and tribe members and of preventing feuds from erupting into violence. Agreeing to move, the Righteous began quietly slipping out of Mecca in the spring of 622. In great secrecy, Muhammad followed in the fall. In Medina he was one among several leaders, but he was successful in bringing peace. He was also successful in leading many to recognize Allah as god and himself as prophet. Some people began to call his followers Muslims, "those who submit," and called the religion Islam, meaning "submission."

Muhammad's success in bringing peace was marred by continuing economic distress for the Muslims. Medina, a farming community, was an unlikely place for urban refugees from Mecca to find jobs. The newcomers knew nothing of agriculture. In fact, they disdained farmers and farming. To them trading was the most noble occupation, but time was required to create a merchandizing business. Perhaps some made craft items, but this work was insufficient. Muhammad's young wife—he had married again—said that Muslims were always hungry during this period. At length they chose to raid caravans, a plan Muhammad likely resisted at first.

War of Muslims against Mecca; Increasing War Booty

During a raid on a caravan, a blunder happened. Muslims killed a man from Mecca. Meccans mounted an army and launched a war against Muhammad and his followers that lasted about six years. At the time of the raid a few Arab tribes had accepted one god, Allah, and they formed part of the Muslims' fighting force. Yet each tribe and clan had its own way of fighting. They did not form a cohesive or efficient force. Arabs had long fought in ways that minimized risk and involved minimal organization. They preferred to appear out of nowhere to raid a village or a caravan, quickly pillage desirable items, drive off or capture animals, then swiftly fade back into the desert. Muhammad, leader of the Muslims, needed to turn these men into stalwart and obedient soldiers. They were Righteous and Submissive, but they were not yet a real army.

In the earliest days of Muhammad's leadership in Mecca, his followers prayed twice a day. This became three times daily after the group migrated to Medina, then five times when the war began. The need to assemble for prayer five times a day enabled tribal chiefs to keep track of their soldiers and made deserting more difficult. Since inspiring the soldiers was an ongoing problem, fiery Quranic verses that threatened lukewarm soldiers with punishment in hell were likely recited to the soldiers before moving forward into battle.

During this period of war against Mecca, Muhammad spoke of the heavenly rewards of the faithful fighter, and he offered horrendous, vivid descriptions of consuming hellfires awaiting reluctant or deserting soldiers. (These are the Qur'anic verses often quoted by today's Islamic terrorists.) Practical, tangible rewards were also paramount. The expectation of booty—often substantial—also motivated soldiers. How else would they be compensated? After the victorious battle at Wadi Hunayn, Muhammad gave four camels to every Muslim in the battle and then gave presents to twenty leading tribesmen. Official lists show 14 men received 100 camels each, and another 6 men received 50 camels each. Muhammad did not forget Allah's share: "Whatever ye take as spoils of war, Lo! a fifth thereof is for Allah, and for the messenger" (Qur'an, 8.41).

Muhammad probably expected that Jewish tribes in or near Medina would accept his revelations because he accepted Jewish prophets. His revelations had many references to the Old Testament, and he also spoke of Jesus and mother Mary with admiration. (One fundamental feature of Islam is that Muslims do not regard their faith as an alternative to Judaism or Christianity. Rather, God revealed His plans through prophets in an unfolding sequence, beginning with Old Testament prophecy to Abraham and Moses, adopted by the Jews, New Testament revelation through Jesus Christ, held divine by Christians, and final revelations to Muhammad, collected in the Qur'an.) When Jews disappointed him by not entering the war enthusiastically on his side, they were punished, sometimes very severely. One Jewish village, however, was spared so that its people could pay a special tax. This evolved into the tax on non-Muslims that became customary in Islam.

Many men, women, and children were taken as prisoners of war. Some were ransomed. Others were enslaved, either sold or given as servants to soldiers. In Islam, slaves who convert are given their freedom, and many made this choice. Some fought at the side of their captors. Such military service by slaves began in the army of Muhammad and became much more common as time went on.

Peace without Slaughter

In 630 the Muslims from Medina and allied Arab tribes defeated the Meccans and their allies. Before Muhammad marched into the city, many inhabitants hastily converted to Islam. However, Muhammad did not slaughter the men or take them prisoner, as his soldiers expected and as conquerors had done since time immemorial. Rather, he cooperated with them, realizing he needed their merchandizing and administrative experience to rebuild the economy. Peace reigned for perhaps a year and a half until his unexpected death in 632.

THE MILITARY ECONOMY OF CONQUEST: 634–661 C.E.

The Muslims acquired allies among the tribes in Arabia through diplomacy, gifts, promises of booty, and marriage to the daughters of chiefs. When Muhammad died, many allied tribes drifted away. A short war against them brought them back into the fold. This campaign was waged by Abu Bakr, the first successor to Muhammad. During his reign of just two years he pulled the tribes into a loosely organized army. Abu Bakr, an early convert and Muhammad's most loyal and trusted follower, was called *caliph*, meaning "companion of the Prophet." He was the father of 'Aisha, Muhammad's favorite wife. Abu Bakr was chosen by a gathering of tribal chieftains and their advisors, as were each of the first four caliphs. This was a rough form of democracy.

The whirlwind of conquest burst forth from Arabia after the death of Abu Bakr, about two years after the death of Muhammad. 'Umar, the second caliph and a harsh leader, commanded the Arab chieftains, who led their men north into settled lands in 634. "In the name of their jealous God the Arabs ordered rulers of the Middle East to convert and martyred the garrison at Gaza." [3]

The Problem of Getting Men to Fight

The loyalty of chieftains and their men was a recurring problem that required sticks and carrots. For example, after a significant defeat 'Umar and his advisors approached a tribal leader called Janir. In return for bringing his tribesmen into the army, Janir demanded booty over and above the normal share. This 'Umar granted, but afterwards Janir never received a top command. Bribes and incentives included grants of land. Lands vacated by conquered people were granted to some of the tribes, but they did not hold these lands very long because 'Umar devised an ingenious incentive for the continuance of military service. 'Umar persuaded many land-grant recipients to relinquish their lands in favor of regular stipends for ongoing army service to be followed by retirement pay. He established a system of carefully recorded stipends paid only to those who were stationed in garrisons established throughout the growing empire.

Under 'Umar Islam Developed in Conservative Directions

'Umar declared that the government of the Muslim empire—the state—owned all land, following the example of Asian rulers who

---

3. PATRICIA CRONE, *Slaves on Horseback*, Cambridge University Press, 1980, 26.

surrendered to him. This practice became traditional in Islam. Over the course of several decades, the garrisons became cities, and Muslims became city folk with anti-rural attitudes. 'Umar was responsible for channeling the development of Islam in conservative directions. Observing the veiling of women among conquered people, 'Umar also fastened that custom upon the Arabs. It is now a tradition in much of the Muslim world.

Although the Qur'an, after it became a book, has many favorable references to persons in the Bible, 'Umar had a narrower view. "'Umar once caught an Arab copying the book of Daniel . . . and thrashed the man repeatedly to the accompaniment of the verse 'We have revealed to you an Arabic Koran' until the wretched victim cried out that he repented." [4]

The Heady, Never-To-Be-Forgotten Conquests and Unexpected Riches

By 646 C.E., a mere dozen years since the first Muslim armies took to battle under 'Umar, Islamic forces had subdued Palestine, Egypt, Syria, Iraq, and part of Iran. The conquests were a thrilling and exhilarating experience for the Arabs. Massive windfalls of loot, plunder, tribute, gifts, and resources suddenly and dramatically enriched all society, including the families of soldiers left behind in Arabia. Tribal chieftains distributed the booty and military stipends. The number of slaves swelled. Some became the property of officers and soldiers—or were sold as slaves—and some became wives of the Arabs. The large numbers of captive children and women without husbands brought social problems, altering age-old marriage and family customs.

4. Ibid., 18 From al Khatib al-Baghdadi, Taqyid al-'ilm.

'Umar instituted a system of recording military service and paying military stipends through tribal chieftains, with those who became Muslims the earliest receiving more than those who came later.

Under 'Umar, the Islamic faith acquired territory by conquest, and so became an imperial state. Historians inform us that during 'Umar's rule, the empire acquired an administrative base by allowing conquered locals to administer their vicinities. Fixed and regular taxation was introduced, and the physical infrastructure of empire, such as canals, waterways, and travel routes, was created or renewed. The old Roman roads, however, were largely neglected. 'Umar's rule (634–644) ended with his murder for private vengeance. After 'Umar's death, a group of male counselors representing the Muslim community identified Uthman, a son-in-law of Muhammad, as the successor.

The Third Caliph; War Booty Declined

During the rule of Uthman, the third caliph (644–656), the Muslim empire continued to expand, including Cyprus, the complete conquest of Iran, the Caucusus region of central Asia, and a bold raid into Tunis. These victories brought considerable wealth, although it was modest compared to what had been taken before. Uthman centralized governance and revenue collection, largely by naming members of his clan to leadership and administrative positions. He also directed the first official compilation of the Qur'an.

Under Uthman during the early years of conquest, early versions of the Qur'an were assembled from the notes and recollections of listeners who took notes on pieces of leather, animal shoulder blades, and the like when Muhammad preached, papyrus not being available in Arabia. When the verses were assembled, the verses on valorous combat and battle were placed near the beginning. One might expect that early revelations about Allah would appear first, but during the years of conquest an emphasis on war verses probably seemed necessary to compilers of the Qur'an to stiffen the backs of soldiers. But alas, in contemporary times this order of verses conveys a potentially bellicose and tragic message.

Caliph Ali and the First Civil War

Uthman was murdered by soldiers who were dissatisfied with the distribution of military stipends. Ali, cousin of Muhammad, was named the fourth caliph, but he failed to avenge the murder of the previous leader and agreed to arbitration. (Ali was married to Muhammad's daughter Fatima until her death, then had other wives.) This course of action cost him support among those valuing tribal traditions, and the First Civil War broke out. Ali won the "Battle of the Camel" in which 'Aisha, widow of the Prophet, encouraged her soldiers by riding her camel into battle until Ali's men cut the animal down. As the war went on, however, Ali was killed by an angry soldier. The victor in this Civil War was a very capable member of the Umayyad family of Mecca.

Ali's followers in the war remained fiercely loyal to his line of descendants, but faded into the background, emerging over a century later as the Shi'ites, or Shi'a, a minority sect of Islam. Shi'ites believe Ali, the fourth caliph, should have been the first caliph. Shi'ites believe that the line of rulers (or, for them, *imams*) should follow Muhammad's lineage through Ali. Other caliphs are, in this view, usurpers.

Their supreme religious leader was an *imam*. Today most Shi'ites recognize 12 legitimate *imams*. The eleventh *imam* died in 874, and his son, the twelfth, disappeared. Since then these Shi'ites look forward to his return as the *mahdi*, a messiah. This group is called the "Twelvers." Other groups of the Shi'a recognize fewer legitimate *imans*, seven or just five.

The deep hurt felt by Shi'ite Muslims that continues today comes not just from the defeat of Ali but also from a massacre twenty years later of Ali's son, Hussein, and his army by a larger force of sunnis. This decisive battle occurred in Karbala in Iraq, which became a holy place for Shi'ites. Hussein's infant son, Ali, survived, so the line and the controversy continued. Although sunnis and Shi'ites have engaged in conflicts in history (and continue to do so at the present time), they have also lived side by side and intermarried in many countries, sharing the basic principles of Islam.

Sunnis try to follow the customs, or *sunni*, of Muhammad, and are by far the most numerous of Muslims. Sunnis believe all four initial caliphs—called the Rightly-Guided Caliphs (*al-Khulafa-ur-Rashidun*)—ruled legitimately because each was chosen by consensus of tribal leaders loyal to the faith. Further, sunnis believe that these four caliphs lived simple and righteous lives and worked diligently for Islam, Allah, and the community of Muslims. They believe the first four caliphs dispensed impartial justice, treated others with kindness and mercy, and behaved as only the first among equals in a community. However, later caliphs often assumed the manners of kings, emperors, and political rulers rather than leaders of a community of faith.

THE MILITARY ECONOMY FALTERS: UMAYYAD DYNASTY: 661–750 c.e.

The Umayyad clan from Mecca emerged from the First Civil War as the dominant group in the Muslim empire. Umayyad rule (661–750 c.e.) became a dynasty that oversaw the conquest of the Iberian Peninsula (present day Spain and Portugal), an invasion of France, and a formal institutionalization of imperial rule.

The Umayyads left conquered indigenous officials in their positions throughout the Middle East. These indigenous officials constituted the lowest level of government. Their rules for everyday affairs prevailed for everyone, including the Arabs. Even so, the Arabs looked down on these locals, did not speak with them, and learned very little from them. Conquest breeds arrogance and disdain in most conquerors. The Muslims assumed they could learn the arts of government by themselves.

Chieftains of the Arab tribes comprised a middle level of government, the aristocracy of the Umayyad period. Distribution of booty and military stipends was their responsibility. Chiefs also met together in a gathering, a *majlis*, with the provincial governor, and they led meetings of members of their own tribes. The chiefs attending the governors' *majlis* passed on information and gifts to their own assemblies, and the process was repeated by the lesser chiefs in their own tribal meetings. Deputations of the aristocracy might be invited to the *majlis* of the caliph. At Friday service tribesmen might confront the caliph. "But the exchange of bloodcurling speeches and showers of gravel which marked the Friday service was hardly a mark of the smooth functioning of government."[5]

At the top level of government were the caliphs and provincial governors, who exercised fiscal and military power.

A Government Based on Favoritism

Governors were kinsmen of the caliph or members of small tribes related to the caliph's clan. Caliphs cultivated their favor with gifts and honors. Similarly, governors sought the caliph's favor, so showered him with enormous sums of public money. However, the governors retained large sums to benefit and bribe their acolytes, minions, and devotees, thereby keeping many people happy—tribal chiefs, potential rebels, potential allies, family, friends, and the

---

5. Ibid., 31.

poets and well-placed who could make or break reputations. Over time, governorships were widely regarded as sources of private enrichment. Also, the amount of tribute and tax revenue delivered by governors to the imperial city, now Damascus, was stabilized and standardized, meaning governors could keep the additional money they could raise. This arrangement enriched governors and kept Arab tribal leaders and their cronies out of the top circle of political and fiscal power.[6]

> Tribesmen learned they had unwittingly signed away their freedom when they allowed the state to take over conquered lands in the days of the second caliph. . . . [Then the Umayyads] made God's servants slaves, and God's property something to be taken by turns among the rich.[7]

The Arabs had dealt an initial insult to local economies when their conquering forces stripped moveable booty from the land. In addition the enslavement and dislocation of many able-bodied men and women from all ethnic groups severely disrupted pre-existing economies.

Tolerance, Yet Severe Discrimination; Slavery

When peace came, Arabs were generally tolerant of people of various religions and cultures, especially when the people at issue had a holy book. Given the circumstances and the customary violence of antiquity, Arab treatment was remarkably humane when conquest was followed by peace. However, Arabs severely discriminated against those they conquered. They discriminated economically and socially against others. Then, the imposition of increasingly heavy taxes on non-Muslims inflicted another injury to the economy.

Slaves were numerous. The Muslim faith permits slaves to convert to Islam in exchange for their freedom. Many slaves followed

---

6. Ibid., 35.
7. FRANCIS ROBINSON, ed., *Cambridge Illustrated History of the Islamic World*, 1994, 14.

that path. Unfortunately, far from their homes and in a depressed economy, they fell into poverty and desperately sought patrons to whom they pledged the remainder of their lives. Non-Arabs of low status also sought to become clients to important patrons. A new client would renounce his former position, no matter how high, in exchange for patronage and protection. Patrons disdainfully viewed such clients as necessary expedients and symbols of their own prestige and success. The numbers of "clients-for-life" became absolutely staggering. This system distanced the conquerors from the vanquished and cut off the new rulers from ancient learning and local insights. It was quite unlike the experience of the Romans, who became students of the vanquished Greeks.

Unfree-clients supplied a disproportionate number of scholars, scribes, and poets in late Umayyad and early Abbasid periods. "Rapidly adopting norms and values of their masters, they and their descendants continued to be despised by the freeborn members of their master's society."[8] Many clients chose to fill ranks in the imperial military. Their enlistment was practical and advantageous because the fielding of effective and sizable militia based on tribal affiliation had become difficult, especially as the outlook for new sources of booty and tribute declined. In addition, the army garrisons were growing into cities, and soldiers had become accustomed to the ease of city life. Many former soldiers, or their sons and grandsons, entered other occupations.

Decline in the Economy of Conquest; Second Civil War

A weakening in the line of Umayyads occurred when the aforementioned changes and economic decline were taking place. In addition, corruption and low prospects of taking booty in new conquests

8. Ibid., 50.

stimulated discontent, and these stresses culminated in the Second Civil War in 684. Although this war merely shifted rule to another branch of the Umayyad family, a transfer of command authority from tribal chiefs to generals was occurring in that period. Indeed, military service to uphold tribal honor was becoming a thing of the past, non-Arabs volunteered for the army in considerable numbers, and many clients-for-life (also non-Arabs) were assigned to the army. The ongoing change in the army from ethnic tribes to military divisions, from informal marauders to professional fighters, became complete. Although a few regiments were made up entirely of free non-Arabs and continued to fight for plunder rather than pay, most Arab armies were becoming professionalized and ethnically diverse.

New divisions under the command of generals now administered the payment of stipends, collected taxes, and provided law and order. Military factions also sprang up that had no programs and demanded no reforms. These "were drawn from the same army and fought for the same spoils; they merely happened to be too many for the spoils."[9]

"The appointment of a top governor came to mean the appointment of a military faction whose members from the lowest subordinates at the bottom to the figurehead at the top all devoted part of the revenue into their own pockets. Dismissal of a sub-governor [by a governor] accordingly came to mean the dismissal of a faction whose successors had few inhibitions in the application of the post-dismissal treatment. . . . The greater the threat of extortion on dismissal, the larger the amount of money embezzled and the harsher the treatment accorded on the inevitable fall. Failure to pay [to the governor] was met by imprisonment and torture . . ." Governors, who were appointed by the new regime that won the Second Civil War, were rarely

9. Ibid., 42.

dismissed as much as seized and thrown into jail . . . . A change of governors was planned with greatest secrecy. If it leaked out the men in office would either revolt or make contributions to the top figure to buy renewal or at least immunity from torture." [10]

Expansion of Empire with Help of Unfree Clients

When the Second Civil War ended in 693, a second wave of expansion and conquest began, this wave piercing into western North Africa, Spain, and then into France. Since these areas were not rich at the time, these campaigns did not attract enough fighting men. Thus, military commanders relied heavily on unfree clients as soldiers. The invasion of France ended in northern France, at Turin, when Franks won a victory in 737.

With territorial conquest at an end in the West, the spoils of war disappeared. New prisoners were few, diminishing the source of unfree, beholden clients who could render military service. In this period Muslims were afflicted with an additional hardship, a precipitous decline in the poll tax. Having no sympathy for landed aristocracy, the post-Civil War governors eliminated privileged estates, fiscal exemptions, and other arrangements in Iraq and elsewhere. The merciless collection of taxes became a painful example of hard-nosed military rule. Governors introduced taxes on produce (*kharaj*), land (*ushr*), and other items and transactions. Also, no longer could a farmer seek a rural patron to reduce or evade taxes. As a result, a great many peasants fled to cities, monasteries, and remote areas where peasants were not registered on imperial tax rolls. As total tax revenues from rural areas diminished, the governors and their tax collectors invented often coercive ways to extract more from fewer taxpayers.[11] Such episodes punctuate the histories of all empires,

10. Ibid., 44.
11. CRONE, op. cit., 52.

whether Roman, Chinese, Mughal, French, British, or Muslim. Islam differed from other empires, however, because, in this era, subjects of Muslim rule could avoid taxes by converting to Islam.

What happens when many peasants take flight to a city "is described in a stereotype episode which recurs at various times and places in the chronicles, in which a tax-collector writes to a governor that the non-Muslims (Christians in the Byzantine Empire; Zoroastrians in the Iranian empire) have flocked to Islam and that the taxes are in arrears; somebody thereupon points out that they have only converted to escape their taxes, and the governor accordingly takes action by rounding up the fugitives in the city concerned, sending them back to their land and reimposing their taxes. The chronicles scarcely envisage any other type of convert." [12]

THE QUR'AN (ASSEMBLED UNDER MILITARY RULE) AND THE TRADITIONS

As noted earlier in this history, the Qur'an began to be assembled during the period when the whirlwind of conquest erupted out of the Arabian Peninsula. It was assembled out of the fragmented notes preserved by many individuals. As a result the Qur'an is difficult to read. A large number of sentences do not have a stated subject, poetic allusions are used, and sometimes phrases stand alone. It is a mixture of history, praises for Allah, descriptions of nature, examples of behavior, threats, rules, and recommendations. It is repetitious and sometimes contradictory.

The first Arab dynasty, the Umayyads, had sent judges out to many locations around the empire, and they had used pre-existing local laws. At the same time they were attempting to include the directives in the Qur'an in their judgments. This was difficult.

12. Ibid., 52.

Since much of the Qur'an is not clear on specific points or its application to specific circumstances, a form of scholarship arose to help explain and apply the Qur'an. It focused on traditions about Muhammad's commentaries, behaviors, and judgments. These traditions were "not coherent narratives but isolated sayings, short accounts of people's acts, brief references to historical events and the like . . . . The components were easily detached from context, forgotten or given a new meaning by the addition of a single word or two."[13] Along with each tradition, the line of individuals who first told it and who repeated it was preserved. Scholarship came into play in making judgments about how reliable the bearers of tradition were, and the sources of many traditions were declared unreliable.

This process began decades after Muhammad's death and continued for at least two centuries. Similarly, Ibn Ishaq's book, *The Prophet's Campaigns*, the first biographical writing about Muhammad, appeared about 150 years after Muhammad's death and survived only in a critical revision done about a century later. "The *'ulama* [clergy] appear with the Oral Tradition itself, perhaps in the mid-Umayyad period (around 710), perhaps before, and the history of Islam thereafter is to a large extent the history of their victorious emergence."[14]

While this scholarship was going on, military events were occurring and governments were rising and falling.

THE ABBASID DYNASTY

Economic stresses and rapacious governors helped trigger the Third Civil War in 743. The outcome of that conflict led to the establishment of the reform-minded Abbasid Dynasty in 751. The Abbasids, although descending from the family of Muhammad and promis-

13. Ibid., 5.
14. Ibid., 6.

ing justice and devotion to Allah, were not well accepted outside of Iran. The founding caliph, Abbas, began his rule in brutal violence by massacring those who helped him to power and all the members of the former ruling family that he could find.

The Abbasids were unique among Arab rulers in choosing to learn from the people they conquered. From the Iranians they learned the arts of government as practiced by the ancient Persians and the establishment and maintenance of effective bureaucratic administration. The Abbasids also raised a new army among the Iranians, specifically among the clans in Khurasan. The efficient rule and resulting peace over a large trade area linked two sea basins, the Indian Ocean and the Mediterranean Sea. The movement of merchants, scholars, and pilgrims followed long-distance land and sea routes that centered on the Persian Gulf. By the ninth century, however, some patterns of trade shifted away from the Persian Gulf to the Mediterranean and the farther reaches of the empire.

A High Civilization in a Period of Diversity

Abbasid tolerance of many religions and ethnic groups nurtured unprecedented prosperity, and immense riches flowed to the caliph in his beautiful new city of Baghdad. Great buildings were erected and irrigation works were restored. The caliph supported the translation of ancient texts, thereby preserving ancient learning for both Islamic and Western civilization. The work of religious scholars was also supported. The apogee of Abbasid history came under Harun al-Rashid, who reigned in the last quarter of the eighth century and into the ninth.

In this period Muslims had shared the stage with other religions and ethnic groups. A tolerant atmosphere fostered this great civilization, but it did not last. As time passed more and more people converted to Islam, and tolerance of others diminished.

By the tenth century some provinces had become largely autonomous, yet the Abbasid dynasty lasted into the thirteenth century.

Appearance of Religious Judges as a Quasi-Government

Building on the local laws across the empire, *shari'a*, the law system of the Muslims, came into existence. It attempted to weave in the Qur'an and the *hadith* (traditions of Muhammad and early leaders), and it spread over the land. By the time of the Abbasids in the eighth century, Muslim legalists had begun to formalize their opinions on such traditions and to express them in the Islamic Law, the *shari'a*. Religious judges administered *shari'a*, covering all manner of religious, political, commercial, social, family, and private life. (*Shari'a* did not include criminal law, reserved for the caliph and his administration.) This law also served to elevate the social class educated in religion, the *'ulama*. The scholars among the *'ulama* became interpreters of the Qur'an and *hadith* and so of their application to everyday life. The details of the way Muhammad lived his life were derived from the same sources, and that body of information is called the *sunna*.

Early on there were perhaps 150 centers where local Islamic scholars formed consensus judgments, representing a consensus of each community and each developing its own law. Consensus judgments came to be acknowledged as legally binding. In the end, only four *sunni* types of law survived, probably partly in response to political pressure. The Shi'a also developed their own law with some differences from the *sunni*.

Some effects of the dominance of *shari'a* will be explored in detail later. Some of the results were limitations on the growth of businesses, limits on the economic contributions of women, the weakening of central government, restrictions on education, and growing social and economic power and authority of the *'ulama*.

The political and social influence of the *'ulama* came to rival that of government officials. Since the *'ulama*, which includes all those with religious careers involved in worship, education and jurisprudence, interpreted the meaning and application of Muslim principles derived from the Qur'an, controlled the education of judges, and served as judges, the *'ulama* became a de facto level of government. They also controlled a solid, unshakable economic foundation derived from the accumulated wealth of pious Muslims who willed business enterprises to Allah and therefore to the keeping of the clergy. Unwisely, in the view of many, the Abbasids allowed the religious judges to become somewhat autonomous.

Sacralizing History and the Rise of Military Slavery

Many members of the *'ulama* held a worldview that looked backward rather than forward, back to the successes of Muhammad and of the first three caliphs. Because Muslims have "sacralized" history they were unable to acknowledge that Muhammad and the early caliphs acted in a less complex, less vast, less institutional, less diverse world. Further, the *'ulama*, impatient with and intolerant of Iranians (who provided administrators in the Abbasid government) denied support to the Abbasid rulers.

"By the 750s Islam had acquired its classical shape as an all-embracing holy law characterized by a profound hostility to settled states."[15] The *'ulama* defined God's law as *haqq al-'arab*, the law of the Arabs, and God's language as the language of the Bedouin. God endorsed tribal law unless he had specifically modified it.

> For a large group of the *'ulama*, the simple state of the Prophet and the first two caliphs in Medina was held up as the ideal from which the Umayyads had deviated, the accumulation of secular and religious power alike being condemned as a presumptuous

15. Ibid., 60.

encroachment upon the omnipotence of God. Kings were rejected . . . while God's community was envisaged as an egalitarian
one unencumbered by profane and religious structures of power
below the caliph, who was himself assigned the duty of minimal
government.[16]

With these views it was impossible to successfully administer a
large empire.

Arabs Muslims, being displaced in the Abbasid administration
by Kharasani (Iranians), began dropping out of the army. For the
next 60 years reliable soldiers had to be hired from frontier areas.
During the reign of Caliph al-Ma'mun (813–833) the formal training
of slaves as soldiers began. In following centuries military slavery
played a large role in Islamic history.

The Caliphate of Cordoba

A second, parallel Islamic civilization arose in Spain. The Caliphate of Cordoba (or the Spanish Umayyads, 929–1021) was comparable to the high civilization in Baghdad in its scope, grandeur, and
achievements. In both cases the rulers were Sunni Muslims. This
civilization reached full flower about 150 years later than the ze-
nith of the Abbasids in Baghdad. Its rulers were a second Umayyad
dynasty, whose founder, with the help of his faithful slave, had escaped the general massacre perpetrated by Abbas upon the Umayyad family. It, too, was characterized by diversity of religion and
ethnic groups before conversions to Islam and the appearance of
strict fundamentalism brought this richness to an end.

15. Ibid., 60.

EGYPT IN THE MIDDLE AGES

The Rule of the Fatimids, a Branch of the Shi'a

The Abbasid empire became more a region of common culture than a political union when some of its provinces became quasi-independent. The prestige of the Abbasid empire, and the notion of an empire at all, took a bruising blow when rulers in Spain and Egypt cloaked themselves within the title "caliph." The story of Egypt is especially interesting.

Tunisia, to the west of Egypt on the north African shores of the Mediterranean Sea, came to be ruled by the Fatimids, a Shi'a group that had arisen in Iran. (The Fatimids believed their leader was descended from Caliph Ali and also from his wife, Fatima, a daughter of Muhammad.) An ambitious caliph, Muiz, ruler in Tunisia, sent his army into Egypt around 969, and the mission was successful. The conquering general immediately built a fortified palace at Fustat (approximately the location of what became Cairo) for protection of his invading Shi'ites from the local *sunni* population.

Muiz, having spent much of his own capital to conquer Egypt, now wanted a return on the investment. To promote trade and the associated revenue, he ordered the construction of ships and a canal to the Red Sea. The results were extremely profitable for him, and Egypt as a whole prospered. He and his son were responsible financial administrators. The capital city continued to prosper as more buildings, bridges, and a new canal were built. Their leadership encouraged the arts, astronomy, and other sciences, as well as writers, artists, and poets. Muslim scholars created a new library. A new center of high culture had developed.

Unfortunately, later Fatimid caliphs were incompetent, even half mad. The third caliph was a dreadful eccentric who only went out at night, and the fourth ruler, a grotesquely cruel man, imprisoned a large group of women he invited to a party until they starved to death. It was in his reign, in 1009, that Egyptians in Jerusalem attacked Christian pilgrims, an action that set off the Crusades. Previously the West had maintained churches in Palestine, and pilgrimages were peaceful. A chain of events led to the First Crusade at the end of that century. In 1096 Christian crusaders first appeared in Palestine and made inroads against the Turks, capturing Jerusalem in 1099. For the next seventy years the Fatimids in Egypt were in a sort of holding pattern, no caliph having exceptional ability.

As more reasonable rulers emerged, Egypt returned to prosperity. Some years after 1050, the weather patterns changed. The Nile River ran low, and it failed to flood and deposit moisture and nutrients on the adjacent fields. Agriculture failed. The caliph's vast fortune, based on agricultural surplus and a delicate trading economy, was lost. Authority crumbled, soldiers revolted, and merchants conspired. Some wrecked the capital city, stole treasures, and destroyed the library of 100,000 books. Others destroyed irrigation in Upper Egypt or raided the Delta.

When the Nile returned to normal and crops were good, the caliph hired Syrian soldiers led by Badr, a former slave. The caliph began recouping his fortune, and his general also became rich. When Badr died he left his family six million gold *dinars*, seventy-five thousand satin robes, two hundred fifty bags of silver coins, thirty camel loads of Iraqi golden boxes, one hundred gold nails, jeweled turbans, two large trunks of gold needles, and many slaves. The caliph died the same year, 1171, the last of the Fatimid rulers.[17]

17. www.touregypt.net/hfatimid.htm, page 5.

The Crusades Bring Saladin to Power

After the failed Second Crusade, 1148–49, a force commanded by the Christian king of Jerusalem entered deep into Egypt. The Muslim governor of Upper Egypt asked for help from a fellow Muslim, the Turkish Sultan of Damascus, pledging loyalty to him. The Sultan responded by sending a Kurdish general to Egypt, who easily ejected the Christians. The general died suddenly died and was replaced by his nephew, Salah al-Din Yusif al-Ayyubi, known in Western history as Saladin. He became vizier to the last Fatimid caliph in 1169.

Saladin was initially cautious in replacing Shi'a beliefs and practices in Egypt with the dominant *sunni* practices. Indeed, Saladin waited two years before ordering that Friday prayers be said for the Abbasid caliph in Baghdad instead of for the Fatimid caliph. When the Shi'a caliph died in 1171, Saladin expelled 18,000 members of the Fatimid family living in the enclosure around the royal city and allowed local peasants to build in that location. This was the beginning of Cairo. Over the next 11 years Saladin oversaw repairs to a major canal, construction of 5 *madrasas* (religious-legal colleges or seminaries), and a mosque. After 1174 Saladin conquered Jerusalem for Islam and conquered Syria and Iraq for Egypt.

The Third Crusade brought Richard the Lion-Hearted to Syria. At its conclusion in 1192, Saladin and Richard made a truce giving the eastern Mediterranean coast to Christians and the interior to Muslims. They also agreed that Christian pilgrims could enter Jerusalem. (Events changed this agreement almost exactly a century later.)

Many Westerners deeply respected and admired Saladin for his chivalry and tolerance. Indeed, Dante Alighieri describes him as one of the virtuous pagan souls. In the fourteenth century, an epic poem recounting Saladin's exploits was penned in Europe.

Saladin established a brief dynasty, and his close successors were able rulers. They defeated crusaders who had returned to Egypt, expanded irrigation systems, and secured travel and trade. The spice trade flourished and the country prospered despite plague and several unseasonably weak seasons of flooding along the Nile. Eventually Saladin's line weakened. To fortify the army, rulers obtained Turkish prisoners of war from Genghis Khan, the great Mongol conqueror. In imitation of the long and strenuous training of military slaves previously developed by the Abbasids, some of the enslaved boys were trained to be effective and disciplined soldiers. They became known as Mameluks.

The Approach of Mongol Invaders Puts Military Slaves in Power

In Egypt the last of Saladin's line died without an heir. The widowed wife, Shagar, a Mameluk (slave), ruled for almost three months. When the Mameluks insisted that Shagar marry their commander, she agreed, but only after forcing the commander to divorce his favorite wife. When he wanted to marry another wife, Shagar had him murdered. Enraged soldiers threw Shagar out of a window of the Citadel and left her dead in the ditch below. In 1259 the Mameluk military leadership took control of the government.

In Baghdad, the Abbasid Caliphate, continuous rulers since 750, ended abruptly in 1258 when the Mongols, fierce invaders from central Asia, sacked Baghdad. Led by a grandson of Genghis Khan, the Mongols conquered everything before them.*

As the Mongols moved west into Syria in 1260, a very able Mameluk general from Egypt, Baybars, halted the Mongol advance. Mameluk armies also expelled the Crusaders from the region. Baybars had a sizable, efficient military force at the ready. He had created a self-perpetuating military caste of 40,000 slaves continually

* After they had settled down for a few decades the Mongols became Muslim, but cultural rebirth was very slow in coming to Abbasid lands.

refreshed by the purchase of slave boys who were trained as soldiers. By the early fourteenth century the Mameluks had extended their realm northward to the borders of Asia Minor.

Periodic conflict and bloodshed marked the age of Mameluk rule, from around 1250 to 1517. The naming of succeeding sultans (rulers) often sparked partisan violence. Nevertheless, the first half of this age enjoyed commercial expansion and extraordinary artistic brilliance. Merchant princes in the spice trade vied with Mameluk political leaders as leading patrons of the arts. Trade with Venice began. In 1311 a canal was dug between Alexandria and the Nile. The country prospered.

However, much of the Middle East and Europe during this century were shaken by the Black Death. The population of Cairo dropped from 250,000 to 150,000. The countryside also suffered.

THE INFLUENCE OF THE *'ULAMA* AND THE MILITARY CLASS

Islam has no ordained clergy, but it has a large class of people, the *'ulama*, engaged in various religious practices. In the medieval era large numbers of people were attached to mosques and earned part of their living by conducting services. *Imams* led prayers, *khatibs* preached sermons, *muqris* read the Qur'an, *muezzins* summoned faithful to prayer, *muftis* issued legal amendments, etc. The increase in *madrasas*, religious schools, from the eleventh century onwards greatly enlarged Islam's clergy, when professors, repetiteurs, and librarians joined the "Men of the Turban." This was true not only in Egypt but in all of Islam. Under the Seljuq Turks and successor states in the Middle East, the prestige of the *'ulama*, experts on the Qur'an and Islamic law, visibly grew. However, since most *madrasas* were founded by sultans, emirs, and other politicians, the *'ulama* who accepted employment in the schools were viewed by rigorous religious lawyers as having compromised themselves.[18]

Although historians are keenly attentive to the development of Muslim practices, philosophy, and law by the *'ulama*, the military class also made contributions and reaped rewards. The social significance of the military becomes more obvious when one considers who paid for public works and endowed *waqfs* (religious foundations) in the Mameluk period. "A study of great cities of the Mameluk state [which included Syria and Palestine] has shown that of 171 buildings for religious purposes constructed or repaired in Damascus, 10 were paid for by the sultan himself, 82 by high military officers, 11 by other officials, 25 by merchants and 43 by *'ulama*."[19] Similarly a survey of buildings in Jerusalem credits the military. "Out of 86 *waqfs* at least 31 were founded by Mameluk officers who had settled in local society, and a smaller number by administrators, *'ulama* and merchants."[20]

THE SECOND MILITARY ECONOMY: THE OTTOMAN EMPIRE

By the fifteenth and sixteenth centuries, three major Islamic empires existed: a Shi'a empire in Iran, the Moghul empire in India, and the Empire of the Ottoman Turks. The latter stretched outward from Istanbul northward into the Balkans and Hungary, east through Anatolia to the border with Iran, south through the Levant to Egypt, and west from there across north Africa through Morocco.

Just before the year 1300 the Ottoman Empire—centered in Constantinople, then renamed Istanbul—recreated a military-spoils economy akin to the early military economy of the Muslim Empire.

18. ROBERT IRWIN, *Microsoft Encarta 98*, "Islamic World," 40.
19. ALBERT HOURANI, *A History of the Arab Peoples*, Warner Books, 1992, Reference to I. M. Lapidus, *Muslim Cities in the Later Middle Ages*, Cambridge, 1967, 199–200.
20. Ibid. Reference is to M. H. Burgoyne and D. S. Richards, *Mamluke Jerusalem*, London, 1987, 69.

The Ottomans began with raids on Christians in what is now Turkey and quickly established a reputation as a formidable foe. The Byzantine emperor—head of the Byzantine Empire, the successor to the ancient Roman Empire of the east—foolishly hired the Ottomans to help him fight a contender to his throne. Through this activity the Ottomans recognized the rich plunder to be had in the Balkans. The Ottoman Empire grew by drawing its sustenance from military raids and outright warfare against the Byzantine Empire. By the late 1400s the Ottomans occupied the Balkan countries and other Black Sea areas. They succeeded in part because they were ferocious, indomitable soldiers. They were *ghazi* warriors, fighters "who carried out raids upon and warfare with non-Muslims in the interest of Islam." *

The Bureaucracy and Lack of Land Ownership Fostered Rigidity

The three basic features of the Ottoman Empire were "the absence of private property in the countryside, where the cultivator did not own and the owner (i.e., the state) did not cultivate; a powerful non-hereditary bureaucratic elite in the centres of administration; and a professional trained army with a slave component."[21] The Ottomans abolished tribal aristocracy and created an efficient civil service. The Ottoman navy overcame piracy in the Mediterranean, and trade flourished. The Ottomans built beautiful, spacious mosques, patronized the arts, and welcomed European knowledge about medicine and navigation. Refugee Jews and Christians fleeing strife in Europe found safety, and their knowledge and work furthered a high level of civilization. To supply their administration and elite infantry, a system of human taxation called *devshirme* was instituted in the

---

* More correctly, they fought "in the economic interest of Islam." These soldiers were not *jihadists*, fighting "holy wars" against enemies determined to destroy the religion. The people of the Balkans did not threaten Islam.
21. Tariq Ali, *The Clash of Fundamentalisms*, 47–8.

1420s under Sultan Murad the Second. Strong, healthy boys typically between ages of 8 and 10, but sometimes as old as 20, were seized from Christian families and declared slaves of the sultan. The fittest boys were sent to the sultan's palace for training. Others were sent to rural families. By about age 20 or after 7 to 10 years of training, the boys would be assigned to the army or to the civil service. After entry into a professional calling, the slaves of the *devshirme* could own land, but could not become completely free.

The system of *devshirme*, meaning "the gathering" in Turkish, arose from the pressing military needs of a fast-growing empire. The empire needed many loyal, high-quality soldiers in the battlefield and efficient, reliable civil servants in administrative posts. Another purpose of the system was to prevent the development of a hereditary aristocracy which could threaten the status or influence of the sultan. To this end, only non-Muslims could enter the *devshirme*, which was considered an honor, a path from rural poverty to prominence. The system worked exactly as intended for several centuries.

When officials recognized the legal authority of Islamic courts, the role of religion in society grew. Religious-legal experts (*muftis*) and teachers in schools of religion and law (*madrassas*) became part of an official corps paid by the government. Muslim "clergy" also profited from the religious foundations they administered. Although the sultan and his *pashas* could control clerics by threatening to withdraw their subsidies, the *'ulama* continued to press orthodox practices and were not in opposition to the government as they had been early in Islamic history. They remained suspicious of new ideas. For example, the *'ulama* opposed the use of the printing press, thus protecting jobs of the scribes, but greatly reducing access to advances being made in Europe.

Since power was needed to collect taxes in the countryside, military men and administrators controlled this collection. Their subsequently surpassed that of the men of religion. Other taxes and dues, especially urban taxes, were collected by the *'ulama* and by merchants. In the seventeenth century, inflation stemming from profitable business activity in Europe and from the influx of Spanish silver caused many people to abandon farms. As government revenue from rural taxes fell, some tax collectors became corrupt. Inflation and economic flux also meant that the financial burdens of a large army became quite heavy. Also, the source of slaves was drying up because conquests were slowing or ending and because it became harder to requisition young boys repeatedly from the same Christian villages.

In short, the underpinnings of Ottoman success were beginning to erode. The empire was becoming less agile, less adept, and less able to adapt.

The Impact of Western Civilization on the Inflexible Ottoman World

As Ottoman society and government became increasingly inflexible, the Empire became less able to respond to challenges posed by the growing prosperity, strength, and assertiveness of the West. A reverberating shock came in 1798 when Napoleon and his troops took Egypt and remained for three years. Although the French were driven out, Ottoman power over the next few decades could not defeat Greece in its fight for independence, nor hold Algeria and Tunisia against the inroads of France. The Ottoman Empire continued to shrink in the 1800s. After France took Algeria, in due course Egypt and Tunisia fell under European control, and then Morocco and Libya. Russia took Bulgaria.

Elsewhere in the Empire, Europeans were investing in various projects and businesses. As industrial methods were introduced, people in older, traditional industries, such as textiles, experienced a loss of power, influence, and status. Just as buggy makers and whip makers suffered with the appearance of new forms of transportation in the West, the arrival of new modes of transportation diminished the importance of the camel and all people involved in this ancient business.

The sultan's Land Law of 1858 clarified that land belonged to the state, but cultivators could obtain title to land, giving them the right to sell or will to heirs the rights to cultivation. Unfortunately, land near the cities tended to fall into hands of urban families who understood the necessary paperwork, and the sultan became the largest land holder. Land more distant from cities came under the control of the leading family of each tribe or the control of merchants or money lenders acting as land agents.[22]

Egypt, nominally part of the Ottoman domain, passed a series of land laws for full private land ownership, but this also created a class of large landowners, the ruler favoring relatives, high officials, and important village families. Some small owners lost their land through debt. Small owners continued to divide land into inheritances that could not support a family. By World War I, one fifth of Egypt's working population was landless, and 40 percent of the land was held by large owners.

Many of these landowners arrived from Europe and scanned the horizon for investment opportunities. In Egypt the construction of railroads and the Suez Canal loaded the country with debt and caused Great Britain to take financial control, then to occupy it in 1882. Meanwhile, cotton culture was replacing food production and by 1900 Egypt was importing food. By World War I, settlers from France and Italy occupied one fifth of the land in Tunisia and one third of the land in Algeria.

22. HOURANI, 1992, 322–3.

For all of the wealth, power, and influence of previous centuries, the twentieth century heralded an era of poverty, marginalization, declining relevance, and rapid change for the Muslim world. A culture of modernity was changing the lives of many Muslims who no longer prayed five times a day nor followed other Muslim customs. Religious studies no longer led to governmental office. *Imams* were no longer as central to the lives of most people, nor as highly placed in government. New commercial and civil codes of law limited the scope of the *shari'a*. Many Muslims, especially in cities, observed that a separation of religion from government fostered a successful economy. Port cities along the Mediterranean were coming to reflect European cities and tastes. Bilingual elites became increasingly open to Western ideas. The public was discussing the advantages of women's emancipation. In Algeria and Tunis, religious foundations under the *'ulama* ended. Land previously owned by the foundation land was given to European settlers. The status and income of the *'ulama* were seriously declining.

THE END OF THE OTTOMANS AND A NEW MIDDLE EAST

In World War I the Ottomans sided with the losing forces, so suffered the same defeat as the Germans and Austrians. The Empire formally ended in the years 1919 to 1924, when it was replaced by Turkey and by nations newly drawn on the map of the Middle East.

In Syria, Palestine, Lebanon, and Egypt, Muslims and Christians continued to live together in peace, as they had under the Ottomans, but now they felt emotionally attached to their new countries. Turkey abolished the *shari'a*, and its use became limited in most of the Muslim world except Saudi Arabia, which clung to the most strict of the four versions of the law. (This is the Hanbali law, which is followed by the Wahhabis.)

Between the two World Wars, Europeans invested heavily in Muslim countries in railroads, roads, agriculture, mining, and to a lesser extent in industry. The increase in rural population caused a decline in the ratio of land to labor, a situation "made worse by the system of inheritance, which fragmented small holdings into even smaller ones."[23] Tractors were used more and more on large acreages and gave the advantage to large land holdings. The worldwide depression of the 1930s lowered prices, and laborers who could not survive in the countryside moved to cities in large numbers. By 1937 one fourth of the people in Egypt lived in cities. Cultivation for the export market increased: cotton in Egypt, silk in Syria, olives in Algeria, tangerines in Tunisia, and so on. By the 1960s the entire area was importing food.

Modernity's Shallow Roots in New Muslim Countries

As the victorious governments of World War I began establishing new nations, the notion of "mandate" circulated and took root in the League of Nations. The successful, prosperous, militarily victorious nations of Western Europe should recognize their mandate, their requirement, to oversee and assist diverse societies, and their geographic areas, as they progress toward nationhood and independence. The League of Nations supervised these "mandates" (rather than "colonies"). Simultaneously, a global wave of nationalism began challenging colonial governments. Such challenges sharpened over the next few decades.

The arrival of World War II suspended progress toward independence. After WWII, several new nations were established in the Middle East. Israel was established in 1948. In the 1950s Egypt, Tunisia, Morocco, and Jordan became independent. Libya, Algeria,

---

23. Ibid., 335.

and Kuwait became independent nations in 1963. For the most part the transfer of authority was peaceful, except in Tunisia and Algeria where European settlers complicated the situation. Small countries of the Persian Gulf achieved independence in 1971. Oman was always independent, Iran generally so, and Saudi Arabia had never been the colony of a European government.

Most countries attained independence through a combination of local negotiation and Europe's colonial exhaustion. In the new nations, ruling families or educated elites took over political authority. Unfortunately, these people of privilege generally did not have the skills or the will to mobilize popular support. Instead, they wanted to preserve the status quo (their privilege) in existing society. "The triumph of nationalism may therefore have appeared at first to be that of the indigenous possessing classes, but in most countries this was short-lived, and the victor was the state itself, those who controlled the government and those in the military and civil service through whom its power was exercised."[24]

Most newly independent governments feared the growth of autonomous centers of private economic power that might generate political power. This left the way open for new political movements. Since Islam promotes an expansive notion of welfare, the young Muslim countries leaned toward socialism. The great strides made at that time by socialist and communist parties in Europe, the Soviet Union, China, Cuba, and elsewhere pointed the way. The Muslim Brothers was such a movement in Egypt, the Sudan, and Syria. The Ba'th party merged with a socialist party in Syria and also became important in Iraq and Jordan. A military party in Algeria had a socialist outlook.

Since private enterprise might be too slow in bringing rapid development, government officials advanced economic plans (some involved centralized planning) often involving land reform. The

24. Ibid., 381.

Egyptian government in 1952 limited the size of estates to 200 *feddans* (an area of about 1.038 acres), lowered to 50 in 1969. This law broke the power of large landholders and of the royal family. Syria passed similar laws and also passed a minimum wage for agriculture workers. The bureaucracies in these newborn governments, however, were inadequate to the task. The Iraqi government confiscated large holdings, but could not agree on what to do with them.

Amid Many Changes, the Burgeoning of Government Property

The productive property held by these new governments continued to grow when they nationalized the capital assets of the colonial period. Governments often nationalized—that is, took into public ownership—banks, railways, telephones, water, gas, and electric utilities. In this way political independence increased the economic power of new governments *vis à vis* their people.

The pools of underground oil were also the property of the new governments. Western oil companies arrived to make various agreements and arrangements for extracting the oil and paying the Muslim governments. In Iran under the symbolic leadership of the Shah,* the democratically elected leadership nationalized its petroleum industry in 1951. Western oil companies refused to buy Iranian oil, the economy slumped, and the next year the prime minister was granted plenipotentiary powers. He seemed about to end the monarchy, disorder spread helped by U.S. agents, and fighting broke out. Supporters of the Shah prevailed, and he then took real power in the state. He used his power to modernize and bring increased prosperity to Iran. Much wealth and all political power, however, remained with the Shah and his appointees thereby fueling the conditions, almost 25 years later, for the Iranian Revolution.

* Muhammad Reza Pahlevi

(In contrast to the Middle East, some but not all oil-bearing lands in the United States are government property, but the petroleum industry has been privately financed by individual stockholders. Thus, the petroleum industry in the West supported fairly widespread property ownership, rather than augmenting government ownership and power.)

In several countries, army officers took control. In Egypt, Colonel Gamal 'abd al-Nasir participated in a political coup, then displaced the ruling officer to become the president of the country. Nasir nationalized the Suez Canal, which provoked an invasion by Israel, supported by British and French forces. Facing American opposition under President Eisenhower, the aggressors withdrew. Nasir became a hero in Egypt and much of the Arab world in the process. Indeed, the public life of Arabs in the late 1950s and 1960s was dominated by the personality of Nasir. His actions held out the promise of forming a large, united Arab nation, unaligned with either the West or the Soviet Union, and rejuvenated by a genuine social revolution. He became immensely popular with Arab people across the Middle East and North Africa, giving hope for a better future. In 1967 Nasir asked the United Nations to withdraw their peacekeepers on the frontier with Israel (placed there after the previous war over the Suez Canal and subsequent invasion). Next he closed the Straights of 'Aqaba to Israeli shipping. This provoked Israel into a war which Egypt and its allies lost. Thus, Nasirism became a severe disappointment to Arabs.

The Failure to Protect Private Ownership of Productive Property

The rapid changes that took place in the mid-twentieth century and in years that followed at first gave hope to people in the Arab world and in Iran. New political and economic arrangements were tried. Independence, nationalism, pan-Arabism, socialism, land reforms, and five-year plans gave promise of relief from poverty and the end of oppression. Alas, they brought disappointment and bitterness. Democracy, specifically voting, the visible incidental of democracy, was also found wanting. Nothing was relieving the poverty of ordinary people, nothing was giving them a voice in government, and nothing was bringing the elite and their countries a prideful place in the eyes of the world. When many, many promises did not materialize, Muslims, thinking they had adopted the actual economic practices of the West, bitterly blamed the West. Or they blamed their plight on themselves for straying from strict fundamentalism, straying from Allah. What was wrong?

Countries in the Muslim world thought they had adopted modern economic methods. They had failed, however, to put in place what might be called the "economic infrastructure" used across the world in all truly prosperous countries. At the basic level this is made up of the rule of law, protection of private property, detailed registration of private property, and an honest civil service that registers ownership of business enterprises without exacting graft and forcing businesses into the "informal economy." In prosperous countries the administration of the rule of law is predictable and free of graft. In addition, governments cease owning and running enterprises, whether extracting or refining petroleum, mining ores, providing utilities and communication, manufacturing products, running farms, or overseeing anything else that produces consumer products offered for a profit. To create an environment that fosters prosperity, governments directly involved in economic production must disengage by giving or selling the businesses, or stock in the businesses, to their citizens.

When rulers are dependent on citizen taxpayers for the financial resources necessary to administer programs, provide justice, and offer military and police protection, they are obliged to listen to, respond to, and satisfy many of the wishes of their citizens. The practice of voting focuses and sharpens this listening and learning. Unfortunately for political responsiveness and economic prosperity, most Muslim nations are not meaningful democracies, if democracies at all.

PART ONE

CUSTOMS AND BELIEFS BRING RICHES TO THE WEST AND STIFLE PROSPERITY IN ISLAM

CHAPTER 1

PRIVATE PROPERTY AND THE RULE OF LAW

Customs of property ownership either help foster prosperity or smother it. Editor Steve Forbes offers the example of Japan after World War II.[25] He reminds us that on December 7, 1941, violence rained from the air over Pearl Harbor, killing men, destroying warships and airplanes, and bringing the United States into war. After four years of desperate and terrible warfare, Japan suffered defeat and widespread destruction. The U.S. government placed Japan under the administration of General Douglas MacArthur. In a few decades Japan amazed the rest of the world by challenging Western nations, not with violence, but with industrial efficiency and business acumen. What accounts for the emergence of their economic power?

MacArthur, with the acquiescence of the Emperor of Japan, imposed critical changes involving the government's treatment of commercial affairs, particularly the establishment of individual property rights and a rule of law. From the Japanese experience we can see a triad of reinforcing relationships: *rule of law that protects private property* fosters *freedom* and *prosperity.*

FREEDOM AND PROSPERITY IN THE WEST; SERFDOM AND DEPRIVATION IN THE EAST

In the presence of widespread property ownership, representative government is more stable and human freedoms are more secure. Frederick A. Hayek, an economist living in Hungary during and after World War II, strongly and fervently advocated this view. He witnessed how relentless pressure by the Soviet Union forced Hungarian society into communism and how the loss of a market economy destroyed personal freedom. His book, *The Road to Serfdom*, opened the eyes of the West to private property as the key to freedom. Hayek points

25. Steve Forbes, "Mideast Miracle?," *Forbes*, 2/16/2004.

out that the system of private property buttresses freedom for those who own property, but it is also a guarantee for those who are not property owners! Hayek declares:

> It is only because the control of the means of production is divided among many people acting independently that nobody has complete power over us, that we as individuals can decide what to do with ourselves. If all the means of production were vested in a single hand, whether it be nominally that of 'society' as a whole or that of a dictator, whoever exercises that control has complete power over us.[26]

Richard Pipes, Baird Research Professor of History at Harvard University, has spent his career studying Russia, a country that for centuries has endured one repressive government after another. He became aware that one of the fundamental differences between her history and that of other European countries lay in the weak development of property. Western historians (unlike Western philosophers and political theorists) take property for granted. In the case of Russia, it is not the presence but the absence of property that is taken for granted. One of the major themes of Western political theory during the past 2,500 years has been controversy over the benefits and drawbacks of private ownership; in Russian intellectual history this topic is hardly mentioned because of the virtual unanimity that it is an unmitigated evil.[27]

Pipes says, "The idea that liberty and property are connected is hardly new—it emerged in the seventeenth century and became commonplace in the eighteenth century, but to the best of my knowledge no one has as yet attempted to demonstrate this on the basis of the evidence."[28] He found that the history of freedom and the history of property proceed on isolated tracks, researched by different people, and seldom do scholars search for relationships

26. Heritage Foundation, *Index of Economic Freedom*, 2003, "Introduction" (quoting Hayek).
27. RICHARD PIPES, *Property and Freedom*, Vintage Books, 1999, xiii.
28. Ibid., xi-xii.

between the two. He decided to try to fill that gap, and produced an important book, *Property and Freedom.*

Antiquity to the Middle Ages

In remotest antiquity "patrimonial regimes" prevailed. The monarch owned and ruled the land and exercised power over land and inhabitants alike. In ancient Egypt, the whole country was the royal domain, even the vast lands turned over to the clergy. In addition, a network of royal monopolies embraced both production and sale of goods. Although perhaps Mesopotamia and Egypt knew something of private property in a few instances, Pipes observes that the marginal presence of private property in land and the absence of political and civil rights are the distinguishing features of Oriental despotisms.

In recorded history, private property first appeared in Greece. The early Greek poets, Homer and Hesiod, describe a place where many individuals owned farms and enterprises. The writings of Plato and Aristotle show that private property was taken for granted. Land ownership was widely distributed, and even artisans were independent entrepreneurs. "An outstanding feature of ancient Greece was the close correlation between ownership and political as well as civil liberty." [29] Wise leaders pursued policies that assured land ownership by small farmers, who made up their army of *hoplites*, untaxed citizens providing their own armor. In an environment where individuals and families owned property, it was no accident that Greece, particularly Athens, became the cradle of democracy.

In ancient Rome, property belonged to the head of each family and was not taxed. Propertied men in Rome voted. Property law achieved remarkable development although it applied only to land

29. Ibid., 102.

in Italy, not to conquered territories. An exception was Palestine, which enjoyed some degree of autonomy. Judging by the parables of Jesus, individual men owned olive groves and large farms and expected hired servants to invest their money wisely. There is no mention of ownership by government.

When the barbarian tribes that invaded Europe gradually settled on farms, they were influenced by Roman law. Roman law became especially prominent during its "rediscovery" in Italy in the eleventh century. Then, when the feudal systems of lord-and-subject emerged, the lord did not have an entirely free hand over his subjects. He was obliged to provide protection. If he failed, then the vassal was released from his obligations to the lord. Disputes over the fulfillment of pledges were settled by courts or sometimes by a trial of arms. These mutual obligations later provided the foundation of constitutional government.

The land farmed by each vassal gradually became heritable. It then imperceptibly evolved into private property, the owner able to do with it as he wished, including selling it. The parables in the New Testiment, read from the pulpit, may have served as a template. Meanwhile, as early as 1000 C.E., Europe witnessed the appearance of medieval cities that were self-governing. Eventually, serfs became emancipated if they left their land and resided in a city for a year and a day. Serfdom began melting away in Europe from the Atlantic to the Elbe River in Germany, a river that marked the furthest extent of the Roman Empire. To the east of the Elbe, cities were economically weaker, so did not attract runaway serfs. The autocratic rulers in these cities eventually fastened serfdom firmly on the land. In Russia, serfs fell into virtual slavery. (The Elbe River later came to mark the "Iron Curtain.")

Russia

In medieval Russia, conquerors utterly destroyed cities where private property flourished, and they gathered all rights over property into their own hands. Thereafter, Russia enters a long era marked by a lack of broad-based private property. Russia's governance moved from centuries of extreme absolutism into monarchical rule that made ineffective attempts to give private property to the people. Richard Pipes has briefly but clearly sketched this history.

A millennium ago a city of property-owning merchants, Novgorod, arose in what is now northern Russia. All political and clerical offices in the city were elected. In order to restrain the power of the local prince, the city charter forbade the ruler, his spouse, and his retainers from acquiring land or engaging directly in trade. The people prospered.

Then the invading Mongols arrived in the 1200s. They transformed the princes of Moscow into their agents and imposed a "patrimonial" government that made no distinction between the private assets of the prince and those of the state. The ruler also could claim unlimited services from his subjects. Since rent from the ruler's lands paid all government expenses, there was no need to convene a parliament to ask for taxes.

Ivan III regarded himself as successor to the Mongol *khan*. He took over Novgorod but met resistance. "As long as the boyars [aristocrats] held in absolute ownership the bulk of the city-state's productive assets, they could not be brought to heel." Ivan III confiscated massive tracts of landed estates, including most of the land of the clergy. Also, Ivan III deported the boyars and merchants, and he shut down the great trading depot of the city. Ivan IV— Ivan "the Terrible"—expropriated all private wealth in the city. This policy was later implemented in all Russian cities. The Russian monarchy's antagonism to private property exceeded the hostility of all other contemporaneous governments. The monarchy "refused to acknowledge as inviolate property even personal belongings." The monarchy also forbade trade in any commodity by declaring state monopolies. These measures essentially destroyed business knowledge, skills, and entrepreneurial talent. As late as the mid-1600s, the average city of Russia consisted of only 430 households and an estimated population a little over 2,000.[30]

Catherine the Great, an admirer of Western European society and a fervent reader of Western European authors, came to believe that private property was the foundation of prosperity. To that end, and to win the support of the nobility, she gave nobles property rights in 1785. She also drafted a proposal to grant similar rights to serfs, but that plan was never acted upon. Unfortunately, the nobles' property rights gave them a type of ownership over their serfs. This nobility-serf connection caused many Russians to view private property as an enemy of freedom and social justice in Russia. The Queen gave urban dwellers property rights, but other restrictions slowed business growth.

Despite efforts beginning with Catherine the Great and continued by her successors it was difficult to end serfdom. Finally they were emancipated in 1861 and land was distributed to them. Land was distributed to communes rather than to households on the assumption that peasants would pay their mortgages and come into possession of the land. But the lack of a specific owner was deeply rooted in Russian culture and presented an obstacle to private ownership. The head of household was never considered the nominal owner of property, but rather a manager of property occupied by the family, and he could be removed by the courts for wastefulness or incompetence.[31]

30. Ibid., 174–79.
31. Ibid., 204.

Lacking broad-based private property, Russia moved from centuries of extreme absolutism (based on the royal monopoly of property) into monarchical rule (still lacking a broad distribution of private property), and finally into modern communism (a government system that again controlled the major types of property). Thus Russia, that is, the Soviet Union, "produced a regime that deprived her people of liberties to an extent previously unknown in world history."[32] In the twenty-first century, Russia encounters tenacious obstacles to broadening the ownership of property: Autocratic rule is emerging, and its economy may again fail.

Western Experiences

The history of Western Europe differs from Russia's experiences. The Greco-Roman custom of private property, necessarily supported by law, underlies the worldly condition of people in Western Europe, certain parts of Eastern Europe, the United States, Canada, Australia, New Zealand, Japan, Taiwan, and other places around the world characterized by economic stability and a large role of citizens in government. During the sixteenth century in Western Europe, it was axiomatic that the king ruled but that his subjects owned. Thus, private property was a barrier to royal power. Importantly, "in the 17th century the term 'property' came to embrace not only physical possessions but also life and liberty."[33] In the English colonies in America, those who led the way and encouraged the revolutionary demand for an active role in government were the owners of farms large and small, craftsmen who owned their shops, the owners of fishing boats and seagoing ships, the proprietors of law practices, taverns, and small businesses, such as silversmiths, tinsmiths, butchers, bakers, candlemakers, and more. For most of these, their labor had to be

32. Ibid., 159.
33. Ibid., 112.

added to their capital to make it productive. When workers became distinct from owners, one's labor clearly became one's property. (In this work this form of property, justly rewarded, is wealth that adds to the counterbalance against property owned by governments.)

Two legal traditions emerged in Western culture during the modern era. The first, British common law, evolved from the bottom up over several centuries. "In this tradition, judges are independent professionals who make rulings on cases based on precedents from similar cases. The principles of law evolve in response to practical realities, and can be adapted to new situations as they arise."[34] Common law came to be used in the former colonies of Great Britain: the United States, Canada, Australia, Pakistan, Uganda, etc. It also exerted a strong influence on the small kingdoms on the Persian Gulf that made trading arrangements with Great Britain during the nineteenth century.

A second legal system, called civil law, originated with Napoleon. This system works from the top down, and it discourages judges from making adjustments to meet changing conditions. This law spread to French and Spanish colonies and to their areas of influence, which includes most Muslim countries of North Africa and several in the Middle East. Civil law "is less well adapted to reality on the ground and has trouble adapting to new situations as technology and society change."[35] Many judges using this law are not free from influence on the part of the state and of the elite.

Beck and Levine, cited by Easterly, rate diverse countries by their enforcement of contracts, property rights, and rule of law. They find that countries under common law rate significantly better than countries under "non-case law traditions."

---

34. WILLIAM EASTERLY, *The White Man's Burden, Why the West's Efforts to Aid the Rest Have Done So Much Ill and So Little Good*, Penguin Press, 2006, 97–98. His reference is the essay by Thorsten Beck and Ross Levine in *Handbook of New Institutional Economics*, Kulwer Academic Publishers, 2005.
35. Ibid., 97.

Islamic Experiences

Islamic economic history contrasts sharply with that of Western Europe. In Islam, the custom of treating land as private property was never adopted, despite the ancient custom of tribal ownership of grazing land in Arabia. When generations of religious scholars sought to preserve the ways of Muhammad and his immediate successors, they enshrined many old tribal customs through their wording of Islamic law, often called *shari'a*. Unfortunately, tribal ownership of land was not among these customs. By then all land in theory belonged to the rulers, and Islamic culture had come to be centered on life in the cities. *Shari'a* has historically governed commercial and family matters in Muslim lands. However, in modern times some Muslim countries have combined elements of civil law with *shari'a*.

The next chapter examines Islamic law and customs associated with private ownership.

CHAPTER 2

SOME ISLAMIC CUSTOMS HINDER PRIVATE OWNERSHIP

A number of customs directly or indirectly militate against individual Muslims acquiring and holding property over a long term. In many circumstances these customs compound and reinforce each other.

In early Islamic history, Muslims were discouraged from settling on farms, and the state was recognized as the owner of land. These practices channeled wealth in land and natural resources to governments. Other obstacles were the prohibitions on charging and paying interest. These bans made borrowing money for creating and improving new enterprises quite awkward. However, *salam* transactions allowed farmers to finance crops by receiving some payment in advance. This arrangement was helpful during the long centuries when economic life was primarily agrarian. Other difficulties include the lack of laws in support of free markets, the lack of fair and just enforcement of laws, and inheritance laws.

INHERITANCE LAWS DISRUPT GROWTH OF PRIVATE PROPERTY

Rigid inheritance laws disrupt long-term family ownership of productive property. In the real world of parents' hopes for their children, these inheritance laws caused parents to direct considerable wealth away from the private hands of their families into religious foundations. At such foundations some of their sons might later play management roles.

During the early history of the Arab conquest of the Middle East and beyond, very few soldiers settled on the land. Over time the number of Arab farmers grew. Sadly, however, ongoing family ownership of medium- and small-sized farms could not occur due to the Islamic laws of inheritance. Under Islamic law it was, and is, difficult or impossible to convey enterprises wholly to individual heirs who might have the interest and aptitude to maintain a farm or a sizeable business. These laws called for a specific division of wealth among the wives and children, and sometimes among other relatives, which diminished the size of farms with each succeeding generation. Likewise, a business in a city could not be kept whole over the long term. Of course the skills of artisans and methods of running small shops or market stalls could be taught to new generations.

Muhammad gave instructions for wills and inheritances in the Qur'an. For example, the Qur'an forbids changing a will after it is written. However, it can be argued that the Prophet was not giving directions for the inheritance of the *capital* needed for conducting businesses and for farming. Instead, the Prophet conveyed these verses at a time when large amounts of moveable wealth were being seized as *booty* after victorious battle. Muslims could have settled on and owned the farms they conquered, but they preferred to exact tribute from defeated farmers. Muslims also became merchants, a minority among the Arab population, and their trade did not require large amounts of capital. The provisions in the Qur'an regarding inheritance require division of wealth, but are confusing:

> From what is left by parents and those nearest related, there is a share for men and a share for women, whether the property be small or large—a determinate share (Ch. 4: Verse 7).

> Allah enjoins you concerning your children: the male shall have the equal of the portion of two females; then if there are more than two females, they shall have two-thirds of what the deceased has left, and if there is one, she shall have the half, and as for his parents, each of them shall have the sixth of what he had left if he had a child, but if he has no child and his two parents inherit him, then his mother shall have the third; but if he has brothers, then his mother shall have the sixth after a bequest he may have bequeathed or a debt; your parents and your children, you know not which of

them is the nearer to you in usefulness; this in an ordinance from Allah: Surely Allah is Knowing, Wise (4.11).

And you shall have half of what your wives leave if they have no child, but if they have a child, then you shall have a fourth of what they leave after any bequest they may have bequeathed or a debt; and they shall have the fourth of what you leave if you have no child, but if you have a child then they shall have the eighth of what you leave after a bequest you may have bequeathed or a debt; and if a man or a women leaves property to be inherited by neither parents nor offspring, and he has a brother or a sister, then each of them two shall have the sixth, but if they are more than that they shall be sharers in the third after any bequest that may have been bequeathed or a debt that does not harm (others); this is an ordinance from Allah: and Allah is Knowing, Forbearing (4.12).

These long verses are hard to follow and apply in a myriad of different circumstances. In the two or three centuries following Muhammad's death, religious scholars and lawyers developed detailed laws based partly on these verses and partly on traditions. The circumstances could become quite complex since, because of polygamy, a man could father scores of children. For Sunni Muslims, a man could bequeath up to one third of his property as he wished to anyone, except an heir, for any purpose. Of the remainder, all the wives together are not to receive more than one third. If the family has both sons and daughters, each male will receive twice as much as each female. If the family has no sons, the daughters are to get a certain proportion, the rest going to male relatives of the extended family. Among Shi'ite Muslims the laws differ in some ways. For example, when there are no male heirs, then all of the estate will go to daughters.

Why did Muslims not object to these stringent inheritance laws? Since no strong class of large landholders existed, there was no well-situated group to complain. Those most affected, active farmers, occupied the lowest rungs on the social ladder. Further, there were very few great merchants whose businesses were based on considerable amounts of capital. In the day of Muhammad and his immediate successors, the accumulation of booty and tribute by soldiers could be divided up without destroying any ongoing Muslim enterprise or farm. Islam did not develop in an environment close to the soil, the principal form of capital. Its clerics and judges seemed to give no thought to cutting farms into plots too small to support a family. It is significant that after the Conquest, the last persons to convert to Islam were farmers.

Daniel Pipes* states that Muslims regularly tried to apply these laws despite widespread maneuvering around them. An attached reference reads, "In Iran, especially, the aristocracy exploited every loophole and even committed incest in order to preserve a fortune."[36] He explains:

> Polygamy exacerbated this diffusion of wealth, for rich men tended to have large families, and so the share of each individual heir was often quite small. No matter how rich the grandfather, two generations later his grandchildren usually received modest inheritances. Unable to concentrate their resources, great families did not often gain a hold on important positions. Islamicate society knew no rigid social boundaries but was a constant flux of persons and families.... Only in religious officialdom, where special skills formed the basis of power, does one find consistent hereditary patterns.[37]

From early in Islamic history, careers that offered a chance of multigenerational family identity and wealth lay in religious scholarship and leadership, not in agriculture or business. Without links to men of religion, elite fortunes could not be maintained over several generations in the productive fields of agriculture, commerce, and manufacture. It was difficult for pools of wealth to build up, create capital for investment, and counterbalance the power of rulers.

36. DANIEL PIPES, *Slave Soldiers and Islam: The Genesis of a Military System*, Yale University Press, 1981. His reference is to R.W. Bulliet, *The Patricians of Nishapur*, Cambridge, 1972. The location is Khurasan. Not to be confused with Richard Pipes (his father), who concentrates on Russian history.
37. Ibid., 98.

EARLY MUSLIM LEADERS BELIEVED THAT LAND BELONGED TO THE STATE

After the tribes of the Arabian Peninsula united, they were determined to preserve what was uniquely theirs—not only their knowledge of one God and Muhammad as his Prophet, but also of a central tribal custom, the right to choose their leaders by consensus among competent and respected men of the larger Arabian tribal alliance. It was incredibly important to them. In this way they chose the first successors to Muhammad.

As the Muslim conquerors swept over Syria, Iraq, and Egypt, they shunned association with conquered people, held themselves apart, kept the peace, and made contact with them only as superiors who exacted tribute from inferiors. Unlike the ancient Romans who learned much from their Greek slaves and unlike the barbarian tribes settling in the fragmenting Roman Empire who absorbed some of the economic skills and arts of civilization from their subjects, Muslims were determined to resist all outside influences.

They did not succeed, however. Silently and swiftly, the Muslims were influenced in a most important way that would undo rough tribal equality and the custom of productive herdsmen participating in the inner circles of government and choosing leaders. The example that Muslims followed was state ownership of all property. In theory the state owned all land, the principal form of productive property. This had been the understanding of rulers and subjects in the Byzantine Empire and in the empire of Persia, regions recently conquered by the Arabs.

The momentous change from tribal control of land to state control occurred under 'Umar, the second caliph, the second ruler to follow Muhammad. Lands that had been vacated by conquered people were granted to some of the soldiers and tribal leaders. However, the income to be made by farming or raising camels and goats was not economically secure, especially when compared to the military stipends the soldiers would receive if they remained in the army garrisons. Furthermore, Arab tribesmen disdained farmers and typically avoided the strenuous, dangerous work of raising livestock. Many soldiers chose to settle in the garrisons. Arab history records that an important tribal chief, Jarir, and his tribe were awarded land. Yet not long after they "were convinced by 'Umar to relinquish their lands to the state in return for a regular stipend or cash gifts, and purchases of additional land by them in this region were also declared void."[38]

In the time of Muhammad the tribes of the Arabian Peninsula held in common grazing land and perhaps some arable land to cultivate when the rains came. These tribes also chose their chieftains by consensus among active and vigorous men. With the great sweep of conquest and the shifting of land ownership to the state, difficulties arose in upholding that tradition of consensus. The first four caliphs were chosen in the traditional manner, but a group disappointed with the fourth caliph precipitated the First Civil War. As a result of the war, a very capable Muslim governor of Syria, a member of the Umayyad family of Mecca, seized the caliphate. This caliph dashed tribal expectations about participating in the selection of the next ruler when the caliph named his son as successor. This created the Umayyad dynasty, which held power for almost a century.

In parts of the Fertile Crescent, the Arabian invaders encountered diverse ethnic groups, including Arabs, who had migrated there centuries before. The Muslim conquerors left these farmers on the land. Decades after the conquest, however, such privileged estates and fiscal exemptions were eliminated as the collection of taxes became more and more merciless. Peasants fled the land,

38. FRED DONNER, *The Early Arab Conquests*, Princeton University Press, 1981, on the Fordham University website at www.fordham.edu, 242.

government revenue dropped, and the larger landowners, who antedated the invasion, collapsed. "But insofar as the land passed into Arab hands, it was the caliph, his family and governors who acquired it, only a fraction passing into the ownership of the ex-tribesmen."[39] This "ownership" of course was subject to change according to the wishes of the caliphs.

These changes led soldiers to examine how they had fared since the conquests began. The soldiers fondly recalled the old ways when each tribe controlled a wide stretch of land, successfully raised camels and other animals, and selected chiefs by consensus. Like Hayek in the twentieth century, these men saw the connection between control of property and election of leaders. They realized when a former generation of Arabs allowed the state under Caliph 'Umar to assume ownership of conquered lands the Arabs "had unwittingly signed away their freedom." Then under the Umayyads God's property was taken by turns among the rich. (The full quotation is in the Historical Background.)[40]

IRREVOCABLE RELIGIOUS ENDOWMENTS TAKE PROPERTY OUT OF PRIVATE HANDS

Albert Hourani, an Oxford scholar, explains how Muslims can ensure that an enterprise will be longlasting. Families can try to preserve their businesses, craft shops, and farms by setting up a religious endowment or foundation, called a *waqf*. Although a family member may continue to run the enterprise, actual ownership is transferred to and vested in Allah, hence is irreversible. The profits could be dedicated to education at all levels, facilities for praying, hospitals, homes for the disabled, inns, drinking water facilities, food distribution centers, animal shelters, etc. Although at various times in history the state has

39. CRONE, op. cit., 1980, 51.
40. ROBINSON, editor, op. cit., 14.

taken control of *waqfs*, over time wealth has steadily moved toward religious foundations.

Such foundations usually are controlled by clerics. Members of families of religious learning often obtained governmental posts in religious and legal service. Through such posts these officials could "acquire control over *waqfs*, including the most lucrative ones which had been established for the benefit of the holy cities or of institutions founded by the sultans; many of these were diverted from their original purpose to private use [of the persons in control of the institution]."[41]

A book published by the Islamic Foundation of the United Kingdom discusses problems resulting when "more and more properties, especially agricultural land and urban properties, are turned into *waqf*. . . . The *waqf* sector operates largely outside the competitive market, resulting in sluggishness and stagnation. As *waqf* properties are exempt from taxes, a growing *waqf* sector would reduce the fiscal resources of the state."[42]

With the passage of time the purposes of *waqfs* may become redundant or even anti-social. At present the foundations can be used to establish Islamic schools and disseminate Islamic literature in countries throughout the world.

PROHIBITION OF INTEREST RESTRAINS GROWTH OF PRIVATE ENTERPRISE

Throughout antiquity and most of history, lending has been a high-risk affair. People with wealth would not make loans unless they could charge high interest. This was true among Christians, Jews, and Muslims. Failure to repay loans ordinarily led to debt slavery for the debtor and/or his family.

41. HOURANI, op. cit., 115–16.
42. MUHAMMAD NAJATULLAH SIDDIQI, *The Role of the State in the Economy, An Islamic Perspective,* 1996, 147.

For Meccans, the prominent high-risk ventures were the long-distance caravan trade to the north or south and the maritime shipments of cargo across the Red Sea to and from Africa. Only goods of considerable value relative to their weight could profitably be purchased, stored, transported through dangerous territory, and eventually sold at a profit. Several merchants would jointly own a caravan of camels loaded with goods. The merchants either had enough money to self-finance or they had to borrow money. Even the wealthy could have bad luck and need to borrow to carry on their commerce. Banking, therefore, developed in Mecca, the hometown of Muhammad, as an essential part of the city's livelihood. His wife, Khadija, whose former husbands had been bankers, undoubtedly was able to obtain credit when it became necessary for her business.

Historian William Watt remarks that Muhammad did not condemn the use of interest when he was in Mecca, the city where many people, himself included, lived by commerce and banking. The Qur'an expresses a preference for charity to a borrower over receiving interest on loans. The Qur'an states that usury will not merit rewards from Allah: "Whatever you lay out as usury, so that it may increase in property of men, it shall not increase with Allah: and whatever you give in charity, desiring Allah's pleasure—it is these (persons) that shall get (rewards) manifold" (Chapter 30: Verse 39). Muhammad shared these sentiments in Mecca, and the view does not condemn paying or receiving interest. Rather, it declares only that charity is of higher value.

Steps toward capitalism were being taken in Mecca, and Muhammad stood at the cusp of this new economy. He severely criticized merchant-bankers for their concentration on wealth and the failure to consider those in need. They retaliated by imposing a boycott around the year 616 on Muhammad, his followers, and even his clan. Perhaps their most devastating action was the refusal to give them loans. The boycott lasted about three years, long enough to drive those who ran businesses into ruin and block others from entering commerce. Perhaps this deprivation and disappointment contributed to the deaths of Muhammad's wife and his uncle, who was also his protector. With his uncle gone, Muhammad was unable to find another protector. In an environment where clan retribution still existed, personal protection provided by the leader of a successful clan was part of an individual's creditworthiness. Muhammad may have known how to conduct a successful trading business, but who would give him a loan?

Beaten down and unable to find protection, Muhammad and his followers moved to a community to the north, Madina. In Madina the followers' economic security depended, first, upon raiding caravans and, later, on military booty. In the presence of such considerable wealth and war booty, Muhammad's attitude toward interest changed. In Madina he first preached against the use of interest. Perhaps he saw a rise in enslavement of men due to their debts. A verse of the Qu'ran, spoken by Muhammad in that period, made a strong criticism of men charging interest: "And they are taking usury though indeed they were forbidden it and devouring the property of people falsely, and We have prepared for the Unbelievers from among them a painful chastisement" (4.161).

Muhammad speaks to creditors who were new converts: "O you who believe! Have fear of Allah and give up what remains of what is due to you as usury . . . . If you do not, then take notice of war from Allah and His Messenger" (2.278). Allah has sympathy for the debtor: "And if the (debtor) is in straits, then let there be a postponement until (he is at) ease; and that you remit as alms is better for you, if you knew" (2.280).

In contradictory fashion, the taking on of debts is approved. "Believers, when you contract a debt for a fixed period, put it in writing. Let a scribe write it down for you with fairness; no scribe should refuse to write as God has taught him. Therefore let him write; and let the debtor dictate, fearing God his Lord and not diminishing the sum he owes" (2.282).

ISLAMIC BANKING TODAY

Throughout history Muslims have borrowed and loaned at interest, even though the practice was frowned upon in tribal custom and is forbidden in Islamic law. Daniel Pipes describes the prohibition on interest as an unworkable, unachievable goal of Islam.[43]

Jerry Unseem describes in an article for *Fortune* magazine how lending and borrowing can be conducted in harmony with Islamic Law.[44] "Islamic banks" began to appear about 30 years ago in the Middle East, their supporters hoping to replace banks dependent on interest. Such banks comply with Islamic law by investing the funds of depositors in ventures that do not involve interest payments, alcohol, or high debt. If the ventures succeed, then the account holder receives a share of the profit; if they do not, then the value of the depositor's account sinks. These *mudarabah* bank accounts are difficult to manage. They require the bank's involvement in business and the trust that companies will truthfully share their financial condition. Consequently, this method does not find much use.

To purchase a car, Muslims sometimes use a similar arrangement called *murabaha*. The bank buys the car a customer wants, then immediately sells it to the customer at quite a markup to be repaid over three years. Any late fees the bank collects must be donated to charity, and the bank cannot penalize a borrower who is in dire straits. Muslims can purchase a house by saving money to cover the entire purchase or by a lease-to-own agreement to be paid off in a stipulated time period. The rent can fluctuate with

43. DANIEL PIPES, op. cit., xvii.
44. JERRY USEEM, "Banking on Allah," *Fortune*, 6/10/2002.

market conditions. Because this casts the bank as landlord, the arrangement is offered by very few banks in the United States.

In his article for *Fortune*, Jerry Unseem quotes Samuel Hayes III, co-author of a book on Islamic finance: "Prophet Mohammad's teachings take very practical account of commerce in the seventh century. It's not up to me to say, but if he were living today, I think he would find some accommodation."

Far to the east of Arab lands, Malaysia is transforming Muslim notions of finance, including the introduction of *sukuk* bonds. Payouts from these bonds are based on leases, profits, or sales of assets. Is it mere coincidence that peaceful Malaysia has not suffered terrorist attacks? "Freedom House puts it ahead of all Arab nations in political rights and civil liberties. . . . Prime minister, Abdullah Ahmad Badawi, promotes his vision of *Islam Hadhari* or civilizational Islam—stressing economic development, mastery of sciences, and respect for diversity as core values of the faith."[45] I comment further on progressive changes and innovations in Malaysia when I address reform of Islam.

INCORPORATION IS NOT USED TO LIMIT LIABILITY

The innovation known as the corporation arose in medieval Europe to provide a legal description of cities and colleges and to the form of self government outlined in its bylaws. The form became a foundation for business practices in Europe and America since corporations can accumulate pools of capital, and the investments are easily transferable. The notion of corporation is not used in Islam. A corporation spreads the risk of loss and also limits the liability of owners and investors for debts incurred by the corporation or for liabilities arising from adverse legal action. Usually, when debt

---

45. Yaroslav Trofimov, "Malaysia Transforms Rules of Finance Under Islam," *Wall Street Journal*, 4/04/2007.

has not been used for the investment, an investor's loss cannot be greater than her or his investment.

Perhaps the corporation was ignored in Islam because commercial law was typically handled by religious judges, men extensively educated in religion but not in business.

SUMMARY

In summary, several important customs block Muslims from developing and expanding the private ownership of productive property:

- inheritance laws that fragment ownership of productive property each successive generation

- the assumption, dating from the period of the Conquest, that all land is the property of the state

- the use of religious and charitable endowments to keep productive enterprises whole, such endowments being irrevocable

- prohibition on charging or receiving interest

- lack of the notion of incorporation to limit liability

- lack of laws to uphold ownership and to require fulfillment of debts and other transactions (In many Muslim countries judges are not free from the influence of those who govern or of the elite. This is an important factor in evaluating economic freedoms, as discussed in later chapters.)

- lack of a well-developed system to legally describe and register property ownership creating "dead capital" (I turn to this important point below.)

"DEAD CAPITAL" IN DEVELOPING COUNTRIES

Steve Forbes explains in his article "Mideast Miracle," how Japan grew into an economic powerhouse. The American occupation imposed changes in the Japanese government's treatment of commercial affairs, particularly the establishment of individual property rights and a rule of law. In his words:

> We in America and the rest of the West take our inclusive, easy-to-access property systems for granted. You own land, for instance, and everyone recognizes it. You can readily mortgage it. Want to start a business? The legal requirements are easy. Want to sell bonds or shares or use other capital-raising instruments? The legal structures to do so are open to anyone who can meet standard requirements. Commercial contracts? They're widespread, and the courts are there to enforce them and to adjudicate disputes.[46]

Forbes tells how Egypt is about to commence a Japanese-like makeover of its society. It "will be initiating reforms that should dramatically transform its economy into a wealth-creating, wealth-distributing dynamo." Most countries of Europe went through these reforms in the past century or earlier. Estonia successfully made the transition from former Soviet satellite economy to free economy by giving prominence to the centrality of the rule of law. Scandinavian countries are models of this enlightened policy oriented to the individual. However, most developing countries of the world—not just Islamic countries, but most of those with a history of communism—have failed to do so.[47]

Property Rights and Access to Property Rights through Legal Registration

In *The Mystery of Capital: Why Capitalism Triumphs in the West and Fails Everywhere Else* (2000), the noted economist Hernando de Soto explains why the prosperity of a country is intimately tied to clear and precise rights of property ownership. De Soto, who for many years served Peru as a government economist and high-level government

---

46. STEVE FORBES, op. cit.
47. Heritage Foundation, op. cit., essays by Mart Laar, Sara F. Fitzgerald, and Robert Pollock.

administrator, developed methods to bring the informal, underground economy into the formal system of legal property rights and legal activity. This program amounted to an intellectual crusade against the Shining Path (*Sendero Luminoso*), one of two main rebel groups in Peru that use terrorist tactics and violence. Shining Path members responded by making at least three attempts on de Soto's life.

De Soto and his group of Peruvian government officials and investigators found that private property rights and laws governing them do exist in nearly all nations of the world. What is lacking is *access* to those property rights by ordinary people. In recent decades many hundreds of thousands of people in developing countries have fled rural areas to settle on government land around the cities. In the resulting shantytowns, *favelas*, slums, ghettos, and the like, relocated peasants and the urban poor build houses and establish diverse small businesses. However, they do not obtain legal registration because cumbersome bureaucracies make the task overwhelmingly difficult. Since the poor have no registered addresses, they cannot secure a title to their homes and businesses, the facilities cannot be used as collateral to secure loans to expand businesses, utilities cannot be connected and billed, and so on. Their businesses operate in the informal underground economy that extends far beyond typical black market dealings in contraband, such as illegal drugs, so includes "ordinary" activities like taxi or bus service and repair shops. Their holdings of buildings, machinery, and inventory make up *extralegal* wealth in property. It is very difficult, however, to borrow on these assets to start or expand their businesses or to invest elsewhere. De Soto calls this *dead capital*. The following paragraphs draw heavily upon de Soto's book, *The Mystery of Capital*.

In attempts to create prosperity, developing countries have adopted the external trappings of capitalism, but not capitalism's internal structures and foundations. With the passion of desperate converts, many governments have cut subsidies, welcomed foreign investment, lowered tariffs, and talked of privatizing industries. But these governments remain impoverished and grow increasingly disappointed. As they fail to prosper, the underground economies endure as a symptom of this failure. Yet these governments have little choice but to continue to don failed and failing trappings, because, as de Soto puts it, "capitalism stands alone as the only feasible way to nationally organize a modern economy. At this moment in history, no responsible nation has a choice."[48]

Many people commonly assume that people typically operate in the underground economy or in black markets to escape taxation. De Soto disagrees, saying that the large numbers of poor have little choice. He says the explanation of tax evasion is partially incorrect: "Most people do not resort to the extralegal sector because it is a tax haven but because existing law, however elegantly written, does not address their needs or aspirations."

De Soto points out that operating in the underground is not cost-free. Corrupt officials may demand bribes, and local bullies or *mafias* demand protection money. These businesses cannot reduce risks by obtaining insurance because no one will sell them a policy. They cannot lure investors by selling shares, nor can they secure low-interest formal credit. They do not have legal addresses. They cannot grow; in fact, they dare not. Their secretiveness might force them to split their facilities among many locations rarely achieving economies of scale.[49]

He strenuously emphasizes the fact that the poor do save. In fact, they have amassed large savings—forty times all the foreign aid received throughout the world since 1945! In Egypt the wealth of the poor is fifty-five times as much as the sum of all direct foreign

48. Hernando De Soto, *The Mystery of Capital, Why Capitalism Triumphs in the West and Fails Everywhere Else*, Perseus, New York Basic Books, 2000, 1.
49. Ibid., 154–55.

investments ever recorded there, including the Suez Canal and the Aswan Dam. "Five-sixths of humanity do have things, but they lack the process to represent their property and create capital. They have houses but not titles; crops but not deeds; businesses but not statutes of incorporation." They cannot easily sell or mortgage their holdings in order to enlarge businesses or create new enterprises.[50]

This situation prevailed in Western nations two centuries ago, an age of *pre-capitalism*. In the late 1700s, Adam Smith had to do his shopping in black markets. France executed 16,000 weavers and importers because dealing in cotton cloth violated the protective industrial code. Across the Atlantic, America was being settled by squatters. The states of Maine and Vermont were created out of the battles over who owned land that was illegally registered or not registered at all. Gold and silver miners set up hundreds of organizations to protect their claims, since no government entity took on that work. Land-law across the United States was a welter of local customs. After the U.S. Civil War, the Homestead Act gave settlers legal title to land after they cultivated it, a simple recognition of what was actually happening as Americans were pushing onto land they felt they owned and were improving it for their own use.

Western nations have so successfully integrated their poor into their economies that they have lost even the memory of how it was done, little aware of the effect of standardized surveying and recording systems. Studying the nineteenth century, American historian Gordon Wood wrote, "something momentous was happening in the society and culture that released the aspirations and energies of common people as never before in American history."[51]

That "something momentous" was the establishment by Americans and Europeans of widespread formal property law and the invention of the legal processes (marketing, buying, selling, and obtain-

50. Ibid., 5 and 7.
51. G. S. Wood, "Inventing American Capitalism," *New York Review of Books*, 6/9/1994.

ing mortgages) for creating capital out of their property. As capitalism extended its reach, it ceased to be a private club and became a popular culture.[52] It is no coincidence that during this period of the early 1800s, the United States extended the franchise to the working class and the poor, and Great Britain created populous voting districts to replace "rotten boroughs" with few voters. In short, democracy expanded as visible, productive capital replaced dead capital.

In addition to registering property and facilitating markets for property, there are other efforts to stimulate business and reduce the informal economy. The World Bank has developed an initiative to reduce obstacles to doing business in poor countries, and it is being tracked by Simeon Djankov and his associates at the World Bank. William Easterly explains what these researchers found:

> [C]ountries requiring more red tape to start a new business have higher corruption and large informal sectors—that is, black markets—operating outside the law. They also find that poor countries shackle businesses with cumbersome procedures to collect debts, enforce contracts, register property, and collect from bankrupt business partners: 'It takes 153 days to start a business in Maputo, but 2 days in Toronto. It costs $2,042 or 126% of the debt value to enforce a contract in Jakarta, but $1,300 or 5.4% of the debt value to do so in Seoul. It takes 21 procedures to register commercial property in Abuja, but 3 procedures in Helsinki. If a debtor becomes insolvent and enters bankruptcy, creditors would get 13 cents on the dollar in Mumbai, but more than 90 cents in Tokyo.'[53]

Every year these authors issue a report highlighting those countries that have most improved and those that have failed.

Bringing dead capital to life, one aspect of overcoming poverty in developing countries, remains to be accomplished throughout many parts of the world, including Muslim lands.

52. DE SOTO, op. cit., 10.
53. WILLIAM EASTERLY, *The White Man's Burden, Why the West's Efforts to Aid the Rest Have Done So Much Ill and So Little Good*, Penguin Press, 2006, 111. His reference is *Doing Business in 2005: Removing Obstacles to Growth*, World Bank. International Finance Corporation & Oxford University Press, 2005.

CHAPTER 3

ISLAMIC EDUCATION RUNS COUNTER TO INNOVATION AND PROSPERITY

Ahmen Goweili, representing the Council of Arab Economic Unity, delivered a dark message in 2002 to a gathering of Arab government officials: The current economic picture for the Arab world was bleak. Unemployment reached as high as 20 percent in the total work force in Arab countries. Trade with the rest of the world was small. In 2001 Arab exports, including petroleum, accounted for only $400 billion, just 3 percent of world trade. Arab exports were not diversified, since oil makes up a whopping 70 percent of their export trade.[54] Of course, oil exports are concentrated in just a few countries.

Attempts to understand these problems have received attention in recent years. Since the Arab world has almost no worthwhile think-tanks, the United Nation took on that role. In July 2002 the United Nations Development Programme (UNDP) published the *Arab Human Development Report* on the 22 nations of the Arab League. A panel of distinguished Arabs—including Nader Fergany, a noted Egyptian sociologist, and Clovis Maksoud, the Arab League's ambassador to the United Nations—examined the economic plight of Islamic nations for this study. The panel placed the blame on several sources:

- unrepresentative governments in those countries

- poor use of woman-power

- inappropriate education

In an article on the *Arab Human Development Report*, the *Economist* magazine asks: "What went wrong with the Arab world? Why is it so stuck behind the times?"[55] The *Economist* continues: "Endowed

---

54. *St. Paul Pioneer Press*, "Economic Outlook Bleak for Arab Countries," 12/19/2002.
55. *Economist*, "Self-Doomed to Failure," 7/6/2002. Quotations in the next two paragraphs are taken from this article about the Arab Development Report.

with oil, and with its people sharing a rich cultural, religious and linguistic heritage, why is it an area where the young, burdened by joblessness and stifled by conservative religious tradition, are said to want to get out of the place as soon as they can?"

The *Arab Human Development Report* states that in 1999 the 280 million citizens of the Arab League nations—about the population of the United States—produced a combined gross domestic product of $531.2 billion, less than that of Spain and its population of 39 million people. Over the past 20 years, the average annual growth rate of Arab League countries has hovered around one-half of one percent. Twenty percent of Arab League citizens live on less than $2 a day, a situation made more difficult by the fast-growing populations and high unemployment rates. However, there is less *abject poverty*, meaning an income amounting to less than $1 a day, than in any other developing region. This "safety net" condition arises in part from the significant tradition among Arab and Islamic peoples of giving charitably to the destitute.

Authors of the *Arab Human Development Report* place part of the blame for the plight of Arab countries on their unrepresentative governments. Although elections are held and human-rights conventions are signed, political leaders once in power usually give up authority only when they die. Moreover, according to the *Economist,* "People are given jobs not because of what they know, but because of whom they know. The result, all too often, is an unmoving, unresponsive central authority and an incompetent public administration."

Another deficit discussed by the *Arab Human Development Report* is the failure to make good use of woman-power. Women are not full citizens. This is a waste. The authors, underscoring the lack of concern for women in Arab countries, could not measure the empowerment of women in eight countries because the data is unavailable and probably uncollected.

The *Arab Human Development Report* identifies a third crucial problem, the knowledge deficit. Although these countries spend a high percentage of their gross domestic product (GDP) on education, illiteracy remains high, and there is a mismatch with the needs of the labor market. Arabs contribute little to scientific research and technology, and the environment continues to be unfriendly to intellectual achievement.

Ownership or control of productive property has little value if humans do not use it skillfully and knowledgeably. A swath of fertile land amounts to little without an experienced farmer who is able to obtain credit to purchase seeds, who has learned what crops to plant, how to fertilize the soil, how to water the plants, how to control weeds, when to harvest, how to process or refine, how to value what has been produced, and how bring it to market. Likewise a craft shop without the craftsmen, a ship without sailors, a forge without a blacksmith, a hospital without health professionals, a factory without managers and workers, an oil field without highly trained engineers and technicians, all have little or no value. As the knowledge and skills that workers possess improve, then the greater the value of the property.

Most economic sectors in non-Muslim countries are improved by knowledge of science and technology. Many businesses owe their creation and existence to scientific discoveries and technological innovation. The *Economist* comments that the authors of the *Arab Human Development Report* carefully avoid examining the part Islam plays in Arab economic conditions. For example, the authors of the *AHDR* don't mention that most education is controlled by clerics. Consequently, the *Economist* observes:

> From their school days onward, Arabs are instructed that they should not defy tradition, that they should respect authority, that truth should be sought in the text and not in experience. 'The role of

thought', wrote a Syrian intellectual, 'is to explain and transmit . . . and not to search and question.'

Such tenets . . . hold sway, discouraging critical thought and innovation and helping to produce a great army of young Arabs, jobless, unskilled and embittered, cut off from changing their own societies by democratic means. Islam at least offers them a little self-respect. With so many paths closed to them, some are now turning their dangerous anger on the western world. [56]

THE REJECTION OF INNOVATION

Civilization was born in the ancient Middle East by landmark advances in agriculture, domestication of animals, commerce, science, and technology. These societies developed coined money, writing, and business innovations such as credit and the keeping of accounts. As civilizations flowered in the Middle East, Persia, India, Greece, Rome, and China, they improved techniques in agriculture, astronomy, medicine, metallurgy, and transportation. In the seventh century, nomadic tribesmen swept out of Arabia, a region with no written history and little literacy, to subdue adjacent civilizations. Victorious Muslims, although a minority of the population, provided peace that nurtured prosperity. One hundred and fifty years later, a brilliant Arabic civilization arose in the region of current-day Iraq and Iran, where the rulers supported translation of the ancient works of Indian, Persian, and Greek philosophy and science. Muslims added to the store of knowledge in mathematics, medicine, botany, astronomy, architecture, and agriculture, and this knowledge spread throughout Islamic lands.

Among the works translated were those of the Greek philosopher, Aristotle, who developed rules of logic which could lead to truths that one can demonstrate. This method entered into the consciousness of Arab scholars. Philosophy in ancient and medieval times in-

56. Ibid., 20.

cluded all of science, and it intruded into theology: concerns about the nature of God, good and evil, and free will. Those debating these topics often used logic and rationality. However, some saw logic as a threat to religion and a direct challenge to the notion that only revelation illuminates truth. Over time, this view prevailed, and revelation eclipsed logic as a source of truth and knowledge. The source of revelation of course is the Qur'an.

Yet the Qur'an is not easy to understand, and the book contains contradictions. Many sentences are incomplete or grammatically confusing. For clarification, the Muslim community required examples to illustrate the revealed principles, examples of how to live a proper life. The life of Muhammad and the early community provide rich, revered examples. For about 200 years after Muhammad's death, the Muslim community collected such stories and traditions and accepted or discarded them as seemed appropriate. Due to the drive to imitate Muhammad's behavior, as illustrated in elaborate detail in this body of traditions, the Islamic faith permeated every area of life for devout Muslims. However, sad to say, Islam's presence in daily life has become rigid and unyielding.

Mohammad Arkoun, a modern Muslim scholar, explains.

> Muhammad put a political order in place in which every judicial-political decision [that he made] took its justification and finality from a living relationship with God. This God was not an abstraction or a vision but a living actor doing and speaking through ritual conduct and exemplary recitation. [57]

> Since tradition recapitulates for the Community of Believers all propositions of truth, all values, all norms of conduct revealed by God and taught by the Prophet, nothing can be added from outside. Any practice or new thought not sanctioned by the tradition must be rejected as an innovation (bid'a). [58]

---

57. MOHAMMAD ARKOUN, *Rethinking Islam, Common Questions, Uncommon Answers*, translated from the French and edited by Robert D. Lee, Westview Press, 1994, 23.
58. Ibid., 50.

The fear of innovation was always operative. As Albert Hourani explained, "During the centuries of Ottoman rule [a Muslim Turkish empire lasting from the fourteenth to the twentieth centuries] there had been no advance in technology and a decline in the level of scientific knowledge and understanding." [59]

In early modern times—the sixteenth and seventeenth centuries—the Ottoman Empire primarily valued applied knowledge, select scientific and technical knowledge from other countries that could be put to immediate use. It was quick to use gunpowder and cannons and to study military sciences regarding firearms. Initially Ottoman armies were formidable foes, equal or superior to those in the Balkans and Eastern Europe, and the Ottoman navy seized control of the Mediterranean. This advantage evaporated as, over passing centuries, Ottomans failed to keep pace in sciences and related fields. For example, the printing press was kept out of the Ottoman domain in order to preserve jobs for the scribes and to encourage calligraphy. The theories of Copernicus, dating from the early 1500s, merited only brief mention in Muslim literature almost 200 years later, and advances in European medicine became known after similar delay.

Most formal education in pre-modern cultures—including medieval Europe—concentrate on academics that prepare men for careers in religion, law, teaching, and government service. So it was in Islam. Among Muslims, the "sciences of religion," as they were known, prevailed in institutions of higher education. These sciences focused on understanding the Qur'an, the traditions, and *fiqh*, the process of thought that produced Islamic law. Such a school was called a *madrassa*, largely devoted to legal learning and often attached to a mosque. It trained the clerics, lawyers, teachers, and many who served in government.

59. HOURANI, op. cit., 259.

NEW INFLUENCES ON EDUCATION: COLONIALISM, INDEPENDENCE, AND RENEWAL OF RELIGIOUS FUNDAMENTALISM

By the middle eighteenth century, the Islamic world began to feel the effects of progress made by Europeans in transportation, exploration, and science. Trade between Europe and the Middle East grew more robust, and the influence of Europeans slowly and eventually turned into domination. For example, the French captured Egypt in 1799 and held it for about 3 years. Similarly, the French entered Algeria in the late 1830s and made it a colony around 1850; Tunisia soon followed. European countries established colonies, which introduced profound changes in education. According to Hourani, by the late nineteenth century the Euro-imposed schooling systems were creating a new class of "educated" citizens.

Many types of schools were created. Muslim voluntary organizations established some modern schools, and Christian groups and missions created their own schools. Catholic schools run by nuns were favored by Muslims for their girls. Government-sponsored schools offered specialized training for students seeking future work as government officials, military officers, doctors, and engineers. Primary and secondary schools existed in many cities, and boys could advance to study at institutions of higher learning in Istanbul. Cairo was home to a French law school and to a university founded by private funds. In short, a new generation grew up accustomed to reading often and widely. Many people became bilingual, speaking Arabic and either French or English. [60]

The situation in Algeria illustrates many of the tensions created by new educational opportunities. Many French and Italian colonist in Algeria were not eager to see Muslims learn French and gain

60. Ibid., 302–3.

access to prominent European ideas, such as liberty, equality and fraternity. In turn, some Algerian parents were reluctant to enroll their children in French elementary schools for fear the children could become alienated from them and from Arab-Muslim culture. Few Algerian children went on to French secondary schools and universities.

During this colonial era, the old *madrassa* system of education was losing its position in society to the new, Euro-centered educational systems. An education in a *madrassa* no longer led to high office in the government, and graduates no longer controlled the judicial system. New criminal and commercial codes modeled on those of Western Europe limited the scope of Islamic law, *shari'a*. With the creation of new courts, new judges had to be trained in new ways. Even within the Ottoman Empire the *shari'a* was remodeled. A few *madrassas* tried to adapt to new needs, but most failed to attract sons of eminent families. However, the *madrassas* continued to offer opportunities for advancement to boys from poor families and to exert power in society by "articulating a kind of collective conscience."[61] Progress toward freedom in education, however, was not to last. After the First World War several Muslim nations edged towards independence, and most achieved it in the decades after the Second World War. New national rulers typically harmed the quality of education by closing most existing schools or incorporating them into the state system. In keeping with nationalist pride, laws declared that teaching in public schools must be in Arabic and the teaching of other languages ended. Even some universities made efforts to teach all subjects in Arabic. Unfortunately, the emphasis on Arabic raised difficulties for natural scientists, who needed to read and understand the languages of the European countries where scientific progress had been nurtured.[62]

61. Ibid., 211–12.
62. Ibid., 291–92.

Most of the newly independent Arab countries quickly established a great number of primary and secondary schools. Remarkable gains were made in literacy, including literacy among women. The growth of newspapers, magazines, radio, and television contributed to the development and spread of a common Arabic culture. In recent years, however, the publication of books has lagged. The second *Arab Human Development Report* under United Nations auspices highlights book publishing. Arabs represent 5 percent of the world's inhabitants, yet they produce just 1.1 percent of the world's books. The non-Arab country of Turkey publishes more books than the entire Arab-speaking world combined. Of books published by Arabs, 17 percent are religious.

"Reading and writing are impaired by censorship, poor education, religious fundamentalism and war," says the second *Arab Human Development Report*. In Arab countries, strict, socialist regimes in the 1950s and 1960s forced intellectuals to be extremely careful in what they said and wrote and to accept government intervention. Further, economic stagnation sapped readers' ability to buy books. In more recent decades, the dramatic growth of Islamic fundamentalism has placed limits on what can safely be communicated. The lead author of the *AHDR*, Nader Fergany, writes, "A book that aims to find a market in all Arab countries has to negotiate 22 countries' censors. The noose is so tight that very little squeezes through."[63]

LACK OF ADVANCED UNIVERSITIES

The West has produced many prestigious universities in its climate of intellectual freedom. A great deal of research across a wide spectrum of sciences is continually conducted, and the sciences are required subjects for students. Research studies have investigated nearly every field of human endeavor. Truth is sought in every field,

63. United Nations, *Arab Human Development Report*, October 2003.

and many ideas are questioned. In the Islamic world, where fundamentalists hold sway, such universities do not exist. Without intellectual freedom, they cannot exist.

Hamburg, Germany was the site where plans were made to seize planes and fly them into the World Trade Center and the Pentagon. Mohammed Atta and two other terrorists on the planes that hit the World Trade Center found their religious home at the al-Quds Mosque in Hamburg, a mosque often visited by al Qaida recruiters. Why did they seek their prospects among the Muslims in Germany? Atta and others are attracted to Western universities for an advanced education not offered in the Islamic world. It was relatively easy to get into the country and to stay indefinitely, the country having tolerant immigration laws and very generous welfare benefits. These men could live apart from German society, and no one expected them to work. This became an ideal educational setting for hatching terrorist plots.[64]

Currently, Arabs contribute little to scientific research and technology, and the environment is unfriendly to intellectual exchanges with scientists elsewhere in the world. The *Arab Human Development Report* noted the active researchers in various Arab countries in 1987, the articles published by them that year and how many of these scientists were cited by at least 40 scientists in other countries. The results are as illuminating as they are demoralizing. Only four Muslim countries had one scientist who was cited by 40 foreign scientists in published reports. These were Egypt (with 3,782 scientists), Saudi Arabia (1,915 scientists), Kuwait (884), and Algeria (362). The 2,255 scientists of the Republic of Korea issued 5 papers that were cited 40 times by other scientists, India's 29,500 scientists issued 31 papers equally cited, and 17,028 scientists in Switzerland put out 521 papers equally cited.

64. IAN JOHNSON, "Muslim Extremism Perplexes Germany on Eve of Elections: Nazi History Inhibits Debate about Immigrants Living on Dole, Cheering Jihad," *Wall Street Journal*, 9/20/2002.

Such evidence points to the intellectual impoverishment of those Muslims under the sway of Islamic fundamentalism. Absent is concentrated study of science, economics, and accurate information about the non-Muslim world—the factual undergirding needed to solve problems in today's world. Absent also is encouragement to think creatively in the problem-solving process.

SAUDI SCHOOLS, WHERE MINDS ARE PREPARED FOR INTOLERANCE AND *JIHAD*

Cold War struggles between the West and the Soviet Union unsettled the Middle East and other Muslim lands. At the same time the Muslim world bore the burdens of stagnant national economies, high unemployment, and unresponsive governments. In these circumstances some Arab men turned to the study of holy war and the reasons for *jihad*, and they sought recruits. It wasn't long before *jihadists* began to enlist schools in their cause. Wealthy Saudis use their riches to build and maintain mosques and schools at all levels throughout the Muslim world. Naturally they promote the intolerant and restrictive Saudi way of life. They operate through diverse charitable foundations in extending such values into every part of the world they can reach.

In Saudi Arabia and in schools funded by Saudis throughout the world, young minds are prepared to be receptive to violence in the name of religion. Consider Germany. Extremists and terrorists recruit members from among Germans who convert to Islam. Islamic leaders inform the convert-recruits that they may become teachers of religion and have no worries about their financial future. They receive opportunities to study religion in a university in Saudi Arabia. One German intelligence officer reports that men go to Saudi Arabia and come back as radicals. [65]

65. D. CRAWFORD AND I. JOHNSON, "German Muslim's Radical Path Was Paved by Saudis," *Wall Street Journal*, 2/22/2003.

In Indonesia, Saudi charitable foundations have funded numerous schools teaching Wahhabism—the teachings of the eighteenth-century Islamic reformer abd al-Wahhab—an austere, literal, intolerant form of Islam. (Despite being driven out of Egypt and decimated by Muhammad Ali—the man who drove Napoleon out of Egypt—this sect persisted in the fringes of Arabia and blossomed and grew with the support of the British during World War I.) Indeed, the strictest followers of Wahhabism declare that those who do not practice their specific form of Islam may be enemies. Followers of Wahhabism describe themselves as "unifiers of Islamic practice" or as *salafis*, meaning "followers of the forefathers of Islam." Strident Wahhabi views challenge the character of most Indonesians who, living for centuries with Buddhists and followers of other Oriental religions, adhere to a tolerant form of Islam. Sadly, the Wahhabi religious schools offer many poor Indonesian children their only chance to learn to read and write, but in these schools they also learn violence and hatred.

Violence first broke out in Indonesia in the October 2002 bombing of a nightclub in Bali. The following summer, suspected members of a *jihadist* group called *Jemaah Islamiyah* were locked up by authorities. At the time, an editorialist observed, "If this war is to be won decisively, it is not enough to lock up the terrorists. The supply chain that provides fresh recruits must be disrupted. The *Jemaah Islamiyah* enlists new agents among those who have been schooled in a network of Indonesian religious schools, or *pesantren*."[66] In Indonesia, Saudi Arabian money should not be allowed to "continue sabotaging Indonesia's future stability and prosperity."[67] Indonesia should take control of the local religious schools in some way, perhaps through government-controlled foundations.

66. "Carnage in Jakarta," editorial in the *Wall Street Journal*, 8/6/2003.
67. Ibid.

The extremely serious and worrisome spread of Saudi ideas is not limited to Indonesia and Germany. Since the 1991 Gulf War, the Saudis have financed Wahhabi clerics and Wahhabi-run mosques and schools in Afghanistan, Pakistan, Indonesia, Western Europe, and the United States. The results can be seen on the Edgware Road in London or Leesburg Pike in northern Virginia. Journalists have no trouble finding young people spouting the most vituperative anti-U.S. and anti-Jewish propaganda and swearing that they would fight for Islam against the United States. The Saudis are waging war against us, financing the spread of the idea that our free society must be overthrown and inflexible Wahhabi Islam must be imposed by force.[68]

As a result of efforts by Saudi Arabia and the United States to drive Russia out of Afghanistan in the 1980s and 1990s, large segments of the Afghan and Pakistani population became radicalized. The Pakistani government countered this influence by licensing local religious schools and creating a new standard curriculum, but the government has not ended the preaching of hate in Pakistani colleges. After the attacks on the United States in 2001, a coalition of Western countries entered into war in Afghanistan, ending the rule of the Taliban and rebuilding the education system. In particular, Western sources provide education to girls. Subsequent violence in Afghanistan and Pakistan has made some of these advances problematic. The American news media has given considerable attention to this situation. Glenn R. Simpson is the author of an article entitled "Terror Probe Follows the Money" that appeared in the *Wall Street Journal* of April 2, 2004. He detailed money moving from Saudi Arabia to a business in Lebanon to a school in Yemen.

The school's founder, Yemeni Sheikh Zindani, fought with bin Laden in Afghanistan and is a leader of the Muslim Brotherhood in

68. MICHAEL BARONE, "Our Enemies the Saudis," *U.S. News & World Report*, 6/3/2002.

Yemen.[69] John Walker Lindh, the American now serving a 20-year sentence for aiding al Qaida, attended this school. Also, several of its students were arrested by the Yemeni police for terrorist attacks, including the assassination of three American missionaries in Yemen.

M. B. Zuckerman, editor of *U.S. News and World Report*, says, "It is outrageous that the *madrasahs* in Pakistan and other Muslim schools continue to preach hate and that Saudi Arabia, home of 15 of 19 of the September 11 murderers, has done virtually nothing to clean up its colleges of intolerance. We must persuade the Muslim regimes to condemn this new barbarism—before it consumes them, too."[70]

In 2003 the Center for Monitoring the Impact of Peace (CMIP) examined 93 Saudi textbooks published in the previous four years. CMIP found that intolerant values are entrenched in the Saudi educational system. Dore Gold details the problem in his recent book, *Hatred's Kingdom: How Saudi Arabia Supports the New Global Terrorism*. Diplomats rarely cope with issues of education and incitement, but after 9/11 such coping must become part of the foundation for global security.

Despite the Saudis' immense program of turning young minds to intolerance and violence, the U.S. government continues to regard Saudi Arabia as an essential ally. Are we selling our soul to Devil Oil?

INFLUENCE ON YOUNG MUSLIMS IN THE UNITED STATES

Muslim schools in the United States are also affected by Saudi influence. In the early 1980s, Muslim immigrants in Herndon, Virginia, a suburb of Washington, D.C., established the International Insti-

---

69. GLENN R. SIMPSON, "Terror Probe Follows the Money," *Wall Street Journal*, 4/2/2004.
70. M. B. ZUCKERMAN, "Looking Evil Right in the Eye," *U.S. News and World Report*, 7/19 to 7/26/2004.

tute of Islamic Thought. Associated with the Institute are a mosque, an Islamic graduate school, and a mutual fund. The Institute was conceived by members of the Muslim Brotherhood in Switzerland. The U.S. Bureau of Immigration and Customs Enforcement conducted a two-and-a-half-year investigation into the more than 100 Islamic charities and companies in Virginia. The U.S. investigation revealed links among these entities and links between the entities and a political leader of Hamas. Further links tie the charities and companies to individuals who founded and ran several Saudi-backed Muslim groups in the United States and to individuals involved in financing terrorism.

An account of the connections among Saudi influence, Muslim education, and extremism appear in the story, "A Student Journeys into a Secret Circle of Extremism: Muslim Movement Founded in Egypt Sent Tentacles to University in Knoxville," published in the *Wall Street Journal*. The tale will set off alarms in an American reader, because in the highest intellectual settings in Western civilization—the universities—some Muslims use "logic" and their "religious sciences" to advocate the destruction of Western civilization and the overthrow of the United States government, with the Islamic law instituted in their place. The conclusion of the tale, the changed attitude of a young student, also demonstrates Islamic traditions of peace.[71]

The story details the experiences of Mustafa Saied, a young Muslim who came to the United States from India to attend the University of Tennessee. On the campus he was attracted by a campus organization, the Muslim Brotherhood, a group originating in Egypt about 75 years ago. The Muslim Brotherhood sponsors social services and works for social reform, but the Brotherhood is also responsible for acts of terrorism. Mr. Saied, flattered to be invited

71. Paul M. Barrett, "A Student's Journeys," *Wall Street Journal*, 12/23/2003.

to join the Brotherhood, became more involved in Muslim fundamentalism. In public talks he favored extremism and began to lead a religious class at the mosque near campus. In his talks he argued for suicide bombings. After leaving the university he preached at a camp for Muslim teenagers.

Another young Muslim, Assini Mohammad, encountered the same beliefs at the University of Illinois, but he had reached different conclusions. A few years later these two men encountered each other at a Young Muslims conference in Chicago. They engaged in an hours-long discussion, each accompanied by a friend. Mr. Mohammad argued that "the basic foundations of American values are very Islamic—freedom of religion, freedom of speech and toleration." He reasoned from Qur'anic verses like, "O humankind, God has created you from male and female and made you into diverse nations and tribes so that you may come to know each other." Late that night, Mr. Saied says he realized that he and his friend "were out of arguments." He thought, "Oh my God, what have I been doing?" Both he and his companion gravitated back to moderate views.

CHAPTER 4

THE ECONOMIC ENERGY AND CREATIVITY OF WOMEN LIE FALLOW

MUSLIM WOMEN TODAY

Chapter Three describes the *Arab Human Development Report*, published by the United Nations, on the 22 nations of the Arab League. The *Report* and a review panel of distinguished Arabs conclude that the poor condition of women is a leading cause of the economic plight of Islamic nations.

Prosperity is bound to be suppressed—how could it be otherwise?—when women, half the population, are not able to use their individual talents to contribute to the well-being of their communities and their people. This is the case in many countries of Islam, particularly those most in need of economic development. In such countries some women—a precious few—may receive the equivalent of a grade-school, or perhaps high-school, education. Yet this "education" is strongly religious. There may be a small number of women of outstanding achievements in law, medicine, writing, or the media, but such women usually are strongly supported by their fathers. These women do not represent the ordinary pattern of life in these countries.

The failure to empower women has been treated simply as a loss to the labor market, not examined in all its economic aspects. Yet let's state the obvious: Women are able to share in entrepreneurial activities, in managing family enterprises, in establishing and running businesses, in judging financial value, and in making investment decisions. Women are intelligent consumers of many products. And, of course, educated women help oversee and encourage the education of their children, and they look after the health of their families. Such activities increase demand for goods and services and stimulate economic activity.

WOMEN IN ARABIAN HISTORY

In the age preceding Islam, women in Arabia enjoyed a great deal of freedom. Some women even fought actively on battlefields. Among early Arab tribes, families traced genealogy and lineage through the mother's family. Children became part of the mother's family, and inheritances were transmitted through females. Following the customs of this previous age, Muhammad's first wife conducted a trading business, and it was she who proposed marriage to him without benefit of an intermediary.

Times, however, were changing. As Arab men acquired wealth through trade and as wars of conquest brought immense booty, men wanted a family structure headed by males. Changes imitated the customs in the world outside Arabia. One female historian describes the process:

> In transferring rights to women's sexuality and their offspring from the woman and her tribe to men and then basing the new definition of marriage on that proprietary male right, Islam placed relations between the sexes on a new footing. . . . The ground was thus prepared in other words for the passing of a society in which women were active participants in the affairs of their community and for women's place in Arabian society to become circumscribed in the way that it already was for their sisters in the rest of the Mediterranean Middle East. [72]

However, the Qur'an speaks of the sexes as spiritually equal before God and, in some respects, as equals on this earth. But men and women are far from equal in their authority within the family.

> If any do deeds of righteousness, be they male or female, and have faith, they will enter Paradise and not the least injustice will be done to them (Chapter 4: Verse 124).

> I suffer not the good deeds of any to go to waste, be he a man or a woman (3.195).

---

72. LEILA AHMED, *Women and Gender in Islam, Historical Roots*, Yale University Press, 1992, 62.

O you who believe! You are forbidden to inherit women against their will. Nor should you treat them with harshness, that you may take away part of the dowry you have given them—except when they become guilty of open lewdness. On the contrary live with them on a footing of kindness and equity. If you take a dislike to them, it may be that you dislike something and Allah will bring about through it a great deal of good (4.19).

Women may work outside the home. . . . men shall have of what they earn and women shall have of what they earn (4.32).

Men have authority over women because Allah has made the one superior to the other, and because they spend their wealth to maintain them (4.34).

The ancient tribal ideas, however, did not die out entirely. As the Arabs backed away from matrilineal marriage, they did not go all the way. They were blocked by the Qur'an and its recommendations on inheritance, which included wives and daughters. A woman could retain her possessions, bride-price, earnings, and inheritances. Although many women used these assets for the benefit of their families, they belonged entirely to her, and she could make bequests. Similar rights were not given to women in the West until the nineteenth century.

Much of the deterioration in women's status can be laid at the door of the second ruler to follow Muhammad, Caliph 'Umar. He advised Muhammad to have his wives veiled and hidden to discourage people from seeking favors from them, this at a time when other Arabian women were not veiled. Under 'Umar's leadership, the Muslims occupied Syria (including Palestine), Egypt, Iraq, and part of Iran. In Egypt they observed that women, particularly elite women, were veiled and confined to their homes. Muslims soon adopted this practice. In addition, the ill-tempered 'Umar treated women harshly in private and in public, and he physically assaulted his wives. According to tradition he issued an ordinance to stone women for adultery. During his reign many of the major institutions of Islam originated. These institutions were further defined and refined by Islamic law in the three centuries that followed, and in that law the subservience of women was spelled out.

One bright light for women in the history of Muslims emanated from Andalus, as Spain and Portugal were known. The Moors (Iberian and North African Muslims) created a highly developed civilization under Muslim rule. It reached its apogee during the reign of Abd al-Rahman III, who ruled from 916 to 961. Work on the Great Mosque in Cordoba had begun, and the city had running water and about 70 libraries. Women became famous as copyists, teachers, librarians, doctors, and lawyers. The achievements and high culture of the period cannot be attributed solely to the higher status of women. Rather, they arise from the greater freedom given to and enjoyed by all citizens and subjects, including Jews and Christians.

Such opportunities for women were not to last. Ibn Rushd (1126–1198), the great Muslim philosopher known to Westerners as Averroes, made an astute observation on the segregation of the sexes after 500 years. He wrote:

> In these (our) states, however, the ability of women is not known, because they are merely used for procreation. They are therefore placed at the service of their husbands and relegated to the business of procreation, child-rearing and breast-feeding. But this denies them their (other) activities. Because women in these states are considered unfit for any of the human virtues, they often tend to resemble plants. One of the reasons for poverty of these states is that they are a burden to the men.[73]

---

73. TARIQ ALI, op. cit., 66.

CHAPTER 5

RAPID POPULATION GROWTH DILUTES CITIZEN OWNERSHIP OF PRODUCTIVE PROPERTY

"In the three decades since an oil boom showered wealth on the Arabian Peninsula, many Saudi citizens lost their taste for work."[74] Five million foreign workers from Bangladesh, Pakistan, India, the Philippines, Turkey, and the United States fill many of the jobs that keep the economy running, while many Saudi citizens enjoy lucrative sinecures in government or private companies and others study abroad at government expense. Around 1980, thanks to income from the petroleum sector, Saudi per capita income matched that of the United States.

Then a doubling of the Saudi population pushed the per capita income down to one-fifth of the United States. Because over half of the Saudi population was under the age of 20 in 2000, that cohort has been growing rapidly, and unemployment is around 35 percent among Saudi men age 20 to 24. "Frustration among idle youths has fueled not only a surge of car theft and joy-riding, but also Islamist extremism." Now, comments Pope, the Saudi government is trying to encourage enterprises to employ its citizens and to have them enter many occupations that they have been spurning.

The economies of most Arab countries grew in the twentieth century. However, comments Hourani, "Economic growth did not raise the standard of living so much as might have been expected, both because the population grew faster than ever, and because the political and social systems of most Arab countries did not provide for a more equal distribution of the proceeds of production."[75] Both socialism and *rapid* growth of the population were at work.

---

74. HUGH POPE, "Saudis Try New Way to Fuel Economy: Going to Work," *Wall Street Journal*, 4/1/2004.
75. HOURANI, op.cit., 437.

The statistics of population growth became more certain in the latter half of the nineteenth century. In Algeria, the Muslim population doubled from 2 million in 1862 to 4.5 million in 1914; in Tunisia, from 1 to 2 million. In most countries this was a result of better food production and improved quarantine, as controlled by European doctors.

In Arab countries overall population grew about ten times between 1800 and 1979, and by that time a large proportion of their food had to be imported. Agricultural production did not keep up with the numbers of people. With the exception of Syria, almost all Arab countries neglected their agricultural sector.

In Egypt, population growth in the nineteenth century was linked to the spread of cotton cultivation, which benefited landowners and provided jobs. Estimated to be only 4 million in 1800, the population had grown by only a million and a half by 1860, climbed to 12 million in 1914, 16 million in 1937, leaped to 26 million in 1960 and 69 million in 2004.

Discussions of population growth occur frequently in *History of the Arabs* by Hourani, which is the source of most of these figures. The estimated Arab population was between 18 and 20 million in 1800, did not double until 1914, then more than doubled to 90 million by 1960 and in the next two decades doubled again to reach 179 million by 1979. (Iran is not included since its people are not Arabs.)

The decades of the 1940s and 1950s saw very rapid change and stressful conditions. In Syria, the change in population during that time period was 2.5 to 3.8 million, and in Iraq from 3.5 to 7 million. Taking the Arab countries as a whole, the total population, which had been some 55-60 millions in the 1930s, increased to some 179 million by 1979—meaning the population tripled.

The birthrate was dropping somewhat as methods of birth control were spreading—even though not widely used in many countries—and urban conditions led young people to marry later. Among the general population polygamy became rare because few men could afford more than one wife. The increase in life expectancy was affected primarily by a decline in infant mortality. The death rate had gone down from 27 to 18 per thousand, and that of infants dropped from 160 to 109 per thousand.

The establishment of the state of Israel in 1948 resulted in population movements. The fairly large, ancient Jewish communities in the Arab countries dwindled as many Jews moved to Israel, Europe, and America. When other Jewish immigrants arrived in Israel from Europe and from Arab countries, the population of Israel grew from 750,000 thousand to 1.9 million. Some Palestinians left Israel, many going to Jordan. The Jordanian city of Amman, with only 30,000 people in 1947, became a city of a million in 1960.

Immigration from the countryside as well as growth of the population swelled the cities. Cairo grew from 800,000 in 1917 to 1.3 million in 1937, then to over 3 million in 1960. In this period Baghdad, with half a million people, became a city with three times that population. In Palestine, the Arab population of the five largest towns more than doubled in 20 years. By the mid-1970s around half of the Arab population lived in cities: over 50 percent in Kuwait, Saudi Arabia, Lebanon, Jordan, and Algeria, and between 40 and 50 percent in Egypt, Tunisia, Libya, and Syria.

In the period 1975 to 1995, cities grew into "urban agglomerations." Baghdad increased over 50 percent and the smaller Iraqi city of Arbil by 600 percent. Teheran increased 60 percent and smaller cities in Iran by from 110 percent to 190 percent. The population of Riyadh, capital of Saudi Arabia, increased by 270 percent. Damascus increased 80 percent, Istanbul grew almost 120 percent, Cairo by almost 60 percent, Algiers by 125 percent, Tripoli by 175 percent, Casablanca by 75 percent, and Tunisia almost doubled.

Newcomers to the cities often settled on adjoining vacant land and lived in inadequate housing without city services of water, sewage, electricity, etc. Many were unemployed and also suffered from weakened interaction with their families and clans. Such family ties had supported them and given them direction in their rural homes. Hourani summarizes: "The nature of economic growth, and of rapid urbanization, led to a greater and more obvious polarization of society than had previously existed."[76]

ULTRA-RAPID POPULATION GROWTH, A HAZARDOUS REPERCUSSION FROM THE REPRESSION OF WOMEN?

Today in many Muslim lands women are veiled and confined to their homes. Their rights are curtailed and opportunities are limited. In these circumstances many women will produce very large families. This is what they know of life, and, after all, the birth of a baby can bring joy and attention to the mother. A Muslim woman also is motivated by the fact that a son might offer her greater security later in life than her husband, who can divorce her at will with no further responsibility. Surely there is a connection between the constricted lives of many Muslim women and rapid population growth. One effect of that growth has been to intensify all kinds of social problems.

In most parts of the world there has been some decrease in the number of babies born. At the same time the drop in the number of deaths has been dramatic! The eradication of epidemics—or the shortening of their duration—has come about partly by putting modern scientific knowledge to use, uncovering how epidemics spread, and devising effective means to prevent or overcome them. In addition, in many parts of the world the general health of people has improved so they have greater resistance to disease. Scientific methods applied to agriculture, medicine, the environment, transportation, and other fields have played a large role in these healthful trends. Agricultural yields are of better quality, variety, and higher volume.

76. Ibid., 438.

Better communication and transportation systems have been very important in distributing food where it is needed.

Islamic lawgivers have concluded that Muhammad did not object to birth control. Limiting the size of families, however, was not pushed by colonial governments and today is not effectively encouraged by Western governments. In the past two centuries, the West has eagerly and very generously shared its methods of prolonging life with the undeveloped areas of the world—the knowledge, equipment, and encouragement for overcoming disease and for improving health. The number of deaths decreased rapidly around the world even though the financial cost of bringing this about was high. Many aspects of modern medicine, water purification, improved methods of food production and food handling, the building of roads and railroads, etc., are expensive.

In contrast, the sharing of relatively inexpensive methods of birth control has not received the same push around the world and has nowhere near the same financial support. In fact, sometimes sharing the knowledge and application of birth control has been discouraged. Sometimes governments refuse the personnel and supplies to facilitate the spread of this knowledge; sometimes funding is cut off by Western governments. Even though the cost of birth control is minuscule compared to the cost of public health measures and modern medical care, the latter have been greatly favored. The inevitable result has been uncontrolled population growth, lowered per capita income, and a harvest of bitterness and sometimes violence.

POPULATION GROWTH OUTPACES JOB CREATION, RESULTING IN HIGH UNEMPLOYMENT

In many countries of the Middle East, unemployment is very high. The following chart shows a correlation between unemployment and rapid population growth as indicated by the percent of population under 15 years of age, births minus deaths, and births per year per 100 women aged 15–18. Contraception use decreases unevenly with population growth.

Unemployment Compared to Population Statistics and Contraception Use

Country	Percent unemployed*	Percent of population under 15	Births minus deaths (est. 2003)	Births per year per 100 women aged 15–18	Percentage of women using contraception
Kuwait	2.2	27.2	19.46	---	---
Qatat	2.7	23.7	10.93	---	---
Turkey	9.3	26.0	10.84	4.4	64
Israel	10.7	26.5	12.03	1.9	---
Egypt	10.9	33.0	18.06	6.5	48
Iran	11.2	27.1	11.28	2.9	73
Morocco	12.1	32.1	16.65	5.0	50
Tunisia	13.8	25.3	10.4	1.3	60
Oman	15.0	42.6	32.87	8.0	24
Lebanon	18.0	26.7	12.64	2.6	61
Syria	20.0	37.4	24.41	4.4	40
Jordan	15–30	34.5	19.13	4.3	53
Saudi Arabia	25.0	38.2	26.94	11.3	32
Algeria	25.4	29.0	12.53	2.5	51
Libya	30.0	33.9	23.34	5.6	45
Yemen	45.0	46.5	34.54	10.2	21

Figures for Unemployed, Population under 15, and Births Minus Deaths are taken from the *CIA World Factbook*.

*The years for unemployment estimates are 2004 for all countries except Qatar (01), Lebanon (1997), Syria (02), Yemen (03).

Statistics regarding women and contraception use are from the "World of Difference" by Population Action International, and their figures are based on 1998 data from the U. N., WHO, and World Bank.

Iran, despite many economic problems, has better measures than other countries involved in terrorism. This probably relates to high use of contraceptives.

Unemployment in Lebanon (18 percent) and Algeria (25.4 percent) are a little "out of sync" with their population statistics. In recent decades both have been wracked by warfare.

Successful Contraceptive Services in Tunisia

Morocco, with a population of 29,900,000, has 14,000 cases of AIDS. Tunisia, with a population of 62,800,000, has only 3,200 cases of AIDS. So reports Bautam Naik, the source of much of the information below. [77]

The low rate of AIDS in Tunisia probably should be credited to the remarkable leader Habib Bourguiba, who began to advocate family planning soon after he was elected the country's first president in 1957, a strategy he continued during his twenty years in office. He prevailed on religious leaders to see that having just one wife isn't necessarily anti-Islam, and in the 1950s the country outlawed polygamy and abortion was made legal. Religious leaders continued to be cooperative. The Friday sermons in the mosques are often dedicated to health, including reproductive health.

The fertility rate, number of children per woman, now is 2.08, which is down from 7.2 in the 1960s. The country pursues social change so that its people will gain economically from the declining birth rate. As one source notes, "With fewer children to raise women have become a big part of the work force. Many women attend the universities." The per capita income rose from $1,430 to $2,070 in a decade.

Under the succeeding leader, Tunisia spends the equivalent of about 18 percent of its GDP on social programs. In urban areas, family planning clinics offer women health services including health education. In rural areas, the government uses mobile teams to deliver health services. Two years ago they began to educate men as well, even those in the most impoverished parts of cities, stressing avoidance of sexually transmitted diseases. Condoms are distributed free in clinics and sold for nominal prices in shops. Birth control pills and morning-after pills are available free to those in need. The

77. BAUTAM NAIK, "As Tunisia Wins Population Battle, Others See a Model," *Wall Street Journal*, 7/2/2003.

government spends about $10 million a year teaching the people about family planning and dispensing birth control devices in all parts of the country.

Tunisia has high quality labor and low costs, and investments result in an annual growth rate of 5% per annum.

POPULATION GROWTH AND CHANGES IN WEALTH PER CAPITA

Population growth affects the sustainability of wealth of a country, and therefore the sustainability of its production. A team of economists and other specialists at the World Bank has calculated the Changes in Wealth Per Capita for many countries of the world, changes that were taking place at the time of their study, published in 2006.[78] They utilize the Gross National Income Per Capita, the Percent Population Growth, and the Adjusted Net Savings Per Capita. The savings figure is based on the gross national savings minus consumption of fixed capital such as depreciation of factories and depletion of soil nutrients and of oil and mineral resources.

They run this calculation for selected countries of the Middle East and North Africa, and it shows that several are on an unsustainable path while others are doing rather well:

Syria, -473; Algeria, -409; Iran, -398, Egypt, -45; Jordan, +28; Tunisia, +176; Turkey, +273; Morocco, +117; and Israel, +268

For comparison consider the following: Venezuela, -847; Russian Federation, +4; China, +200; United Kingdom, +1,725; and Japan, 5643.

78. Ian Johnson and Francois Bourguignon, *Where Is the Wealth of Nations? Measuring Capital for the Twenty-first Century*, World Bank, 2006.

CHAPTER 6

IRAN: ISLAMIC INTOLERANCE DEBILITATES THE ECONOMY

Imagine an experiment testing the effects of Islamic religious law and customs on human economic productivity. The historian Paul Johnson offers some "results" in his editorial, "Want to Prosper? Then Be Tolerant." After examining the records of halted progress, ruin, and waste of oil wealth by Iraq, Iran, Algeria, Nigeria, and Saudi Arabia, he concludes: "On the evidence of the second half of the twentieth century it would appear that Islamic state control is a formula for continuing poverty, and Islamic fundamentalism a formula for extreme poverty."[79]

Iran is a perfect case for closer examination because its economy was closely observed and commented on by Iranians as well as by Westerners before and after an intolerant regime came to power. In Iran, Shi'ite religion is observed in the most thoroughgoing way, and religious judges attempt to hold absolute sway over individuals' behavior. According to a recent report published as the *Index of Economic Freedom in 2002*: "Iran had one of the Middle East's most advanced economies before it was crippled by the 1979 Islamic revolution, the devastating 1980–1988 Iran-Iraq war, and widespread economic mismanagement."

The preceding ruler, Mohammad Reza Pahlavi, who ruled as the Shah of Iran from 1941 to 1979, was moving slowly but steadily to redistribute land from large estates to poor farming and peasant families. By 1966 all large- and medium-sized estates had been broken up to the benefit of four million peasant farmers. Unfortunately, many who did not share moved into slums in the cities. Ongoing programs for distributing land, improving domestic industries, and diversifying export trade impressively enhanced the national standard of

---

79. Paul Johnson, "Current Events," *Forbes*, 6/21/2004.

living. At the same time the Shah decreed non-religious education, equal rights for women, and, in effect, outlawed polygamy.

Unfortunately, the Shah exercised his authority in increasingly despotic ways, relying on the harsh methods of his secret police, Savak. Still, he remained a favorite of the West. The Iranian economy ran into trouble in 1975 and 1976, partly because the national government was consuming much of the oil wealth as the population was growing, as unemployment reached a million people, as inflation rose to around 30 percent, and as people resented expenditures on armaments.

Ruhollah Khomeini—an advanced student in Islamic law at a seminary in Qum, Iran—vehemently attacked the Shah's liberal policies of equal treatment of women by staging a two-day riot.* He was expelled from Iran in 1964 and found refuge in the Shi'ite holy city of An Najaf in Iraq. There he worked out his doctrine of the "Rule of the Jurist," the *velayat*. Khomeini, still a firebrand and a significant irritant to the Sunni-dominated leadership in Iraq, was later exiled to Paris, where he spread his ideas. He published the book *Velayat-e-faqih* on the necessity of a Muslim nation being ruled by "just theologians." He wrote: "If a competent person possessing these characteristics arises and forms a government, his authority to administer the society's affairs is the same as Prophet Muhammad enjoyed. Everyone must obey him." He likened the authority of a *vali* to the authority of a guardian over a minor or a mentally incompetent person. Most Shi'ite clergy strongly opposed his doctrine, saying it contradicted the principles of Islam, but they were not to prevail.

Religious fundamentalists seized power in Iran during the 1979 revolution, sparked in large measure by public hatred of the

---

Riane Eisler in *The Chalice and the Blade* identifies this resistance—and ultimately revolution—as an expected resurgence of male-dominated society (androcracy) acting against a partnership society (gylany), which gives equality to women, extends rights to all, and is characterized by peace, creativity, and a lessening of violence.

Shah's brutally repressive government. Khomeini—now a Grand Ayatollah, the highest ranking title among Shia clerics—triumphantly returned to Iran and submitted a constitution emphasizing the *velayat-e-faqih*. The majority voted against it. Upon the death of an aged and respected ayatollah who opposed the *velayat* constitution, Khomeini and his supporters resubmitted and passed their constitution. Khomeini became the Supreme Ruler. In one of the government's first official acts, the new rulers suspended the Family Protection Act of 1967, which had given women greater equality in divorce, marriage, and inheritance. New laws segregating schools and lowering the minimum marriage age to 13 were quickly imposed.

The new Iranian government did not protect or release American diplomats taken hostage by revolutionary students, became immersed in a pointless and destructive war begun by Iraq, tolerated neither freedom of speech nor press, and publicly executed thousands of opponents, including members of the Shah's government and members of the Baha'i faith, which recognizes the equality of women and men.[80]

The new constitution established an elected legislature, but real political power sits elsewhere. For example, laws enacted by the legislature must be approved by the Council of Guardians, composed of leading clerics and Muslim lawyers. The lawyers were later replaced by government officials. Furthermore, Iran's "Government Principle" number 57 makes the hierarchy of political power crystal clear: "The legislative, executive and judicial branches in the Islamic Republic of Iran are under the supervision of the *vali faqih* and the Imam of the Islamic *umma* [community]." * The powers wielded by the Imam, the chief judge, include appointing all top military and governmental officials and nullifying the directions of the Qur'an in individual family situations.

---

80. Eisler, *The Chalice and the Sword*, Harper-Collins, 1988, 167–168. Cites Fred Brenner, "Khomeini's Dream of an Islamic Republic" in *Liberty*, July–Aug, 1979.
* The *vali faqih* is selected by 83 clerics elected in a general election every 8 years.

By 2004 the raw power of the Council of Guardians was unmistakable and almost unchallengeable. For example, the Council disqualified more than 2,300 liberals running for seats in the legislature. The constitutional weakness of Iran's legislature was vividly demonstrated when only 51 percent of eligible voters in the country went to the polls, a figure formerly in the range of 80 to 90 percent. In Teheran, the capital city, only 29 percent voted.

THE ECONOMIC COST OF INTOLERANCE IN IRAN

The current Iranian government legally institutionalized discrimination and segmentation. In addition to the costs of enforcement, these policies destroy wealth and smother efforts to create wealth. For further details, I turned to Elizabeth Sanasarian, a professor of political science at the University of Southern California and the author of *Religious Minorities in Iran* (2000). The following information is taken from that book.

The religious rationale for discrimination has two sources. One stems from a sense of honor. Many Shi'ites believe the Shi'ite Muslim community is sullied if a member is subordinated to a non-Muslim. The second arises from a sense of purity. Many Shi'ites believe that a "pure" Muslim must avoid contact with non-Muslims and with food, drink, and other goods prepared by them.[81] These beliefs remind one of the "untouchability" found in India, and are not characteristic of other sects in Islam to the same extent. The first results in unqualified men being appointed to management positions; the second seriously impedes business exchanges.

The great majority of Iranians are Shi'as, who are generally much, much more concerned with impure contacts with non-believers than are Sunni Muslims. Ayatollah Khomeini said, "Non-Muslims of any

---

81. ELIZABETH SANASARIAN, *Religious Minorities in Iran*, 2000, 27.

religion or creed are impure." He also objected to having clothes of Muslims and non-Muslims cleaned together. At the beginning of the Islamic regime, an Armenian owned a Coca-Cola plant. He soon fled, and the Armenian workers were fired. Several years later family members were allowed to oversee operations of the plant, but production workers had to be Muslims, since these were the ones to touch bottles that might be purchased by Muslims. [82]

The goal of employment discrimination is to prevent a non-Muslim from issuing orders to a Muslim. The practice is harmful to individuals, groups, and the country. Before the revolution the two largest employers, the oil industry and the government, had many minority employees. After the revolution, these workers were demoted or persuaded to resign and often replaced by incompetent Muslim ideologues. During the Iran-Iraq War (1980–1988), significant numbers of Armenians, Assyrians, Chaldeans, and Zoroastrians fought for Iran and were killed in battle. However, in 1987 laws and regulations excluded these minorities from employment in the professional military and the military industry. [83]

The segmentation of religious and ethnic-religious groups hampers the natural flow of commerce. In 1982 a prosecutor in charge of prosecuting vice singled out an Armenian club and sports stadium because men and women frequented the places together. This caused the prosecutor-general to outline conditions for minorities to live safely in Iran: They must not fight against the government, harm Muslims, drink alcohol or eat pork in public, build religious centers, or commit adultery with Muslim women. Armenians, Assyrians, Chaldeans, and Jews had come to socialize within their own community centers. Yet if an Iranian Muslim were caught in such a community center, it would be closed down for good. Such

82. Ibid., 84–85.
83. Ibid., 87–88.

segregation destroyed cross-socialization and of course prevented potential business contacts. The restrictions were relaxed to the extent that permission might be obtained to play music, to celebrate holidays, or to form societies.[84]

Laws regulated the "blood price" to be paid for damages to individuals. By Shi'ite law, the value of a non-Muslim male is one-half that of a Muslim male. The value of a non-Muslim female is one-half that of the non-Muslim male, or one-fourth that of a Muslim male. Imagine that two drivers have separate accidents: one kills a non-Muslim female and the other kills several cows. The price paid for the deaths of the cows is greater than the blood price paid for the non-Muslim female.

Religious minorities suffer as much as ethnic minorities. Under the current Iranian penal code, the lives of Iranian converts to Christianity have no value. Similarly, members of the Baha'i faith have no value.

The Baha'i religion developed out of Islam and made converts among the general population, hence it is widely spread among the people. In pre-revolutionary Iran, some Baha'is held important positions and many enjoyed greater success in business than the population in general. After the revolution, however, a special animus developed toward Baha'is because Muslims believe that Muhammad was the final prophet and Islam is the final word of Allah. Therefore, any religion that develops after Islam must be inferior. Under the rule of the chief judge, the *veliat*, many Baha'is were dismissed from the work place, arrested, and executed. This persecution diminished after 1985. However, Baha'is were barred from teaching at all levels of education, and Baha'i students could not attend a university. In the late 1990s the Iranian government confiscated the property of many Baha'is.

84. Ibid., 91–92.

The Shi'a clergy in Iran took over administration of education, rewrote the curricula, and insisted on a great deal of religious education. Insufficient attention was paid to sciences and technology, so the country lost valuable knowledge that could benefit individuals and the country and lead to employment. The clergy limited entrance to higher education to those who were recommended by their local clerics and could pass a test on religion. All girls had to wear the Islamic headgear, and their mothers were advised to help by getting them accustomed to hear the muffled words of teachers through the headgear. A great deal of continuous effort and expense goes into a spectrum of repressive measures.

The populations of minorities in Iran decreased markedly, from 1970 to the 1990s. The Armenians (Christian) dropped from 250,000 to between 150,000 to 200,000; the Assyrians and Chaldeans from 30,000 to 17,000; and Jews from 80,000 to 25,000. The population of the Baha'is is not know either at the beginning or the end of this period. Zoroastrians increased their small number of 30,000 to 50,000. These figures are those of E. Sanasarian.

THE ELITE CONTROL RELIGIOUS FOUNDATIONS, MISMANAGE THE COUNTRY, AND PURSUE NUCLEAR POWER

The 2005 issue of the *Index of Economic Freedom* included an article reporting that Iranian President Mohammad Khatami hoped for reform to improve the economic climate. However, Khatami "has been hamstrung by opposition from entrenched bureaucrats who permeate the state agencies and by Islamic hard-liners in the judiciary and elsewhere who value ideological purity over economic progress." A year later he was replaced by Muhmad Ahmadinejad, an aggressive and clever man, and the move towards free markets was reversed and subsidies to the people were increased, even bonuses now given to newlyweds.

Ahmadinejad has said he hopes he will not have to learn economics. Nevertheless, he has responded to Iran's need for power by promoting nuclear power. Their oil fields are not well tended and maximally productive, they need the oil for trade, and they need to import gasoline manufactured in other countries.

The Iranian government plans to build nuclear power plants despite its immense petroleum resources and has announced it will enrich uranium, ostensibly to fuel power plants. Critics, however, worry that enrichment plants may possibly lead to the production of weapons-grade uranium. Iranian leaders have not moved from this course, despite international disapproval and an offer by Russia to enrich uranium for Iran. Meanwhile, the President denies there was a holocaust during World War II, and that Israel should be wiped off the map. He also states Iran's nuclear program is not a weapons program. Ayatollah Khomeini, the father of the Islamic government, endorsed *taqiya*, a religious authorization to tell lies to advance Islam and Iran. This end-justifies-the-means attitude, and a record of broken promises to other governments, makes statements by Iranian leaders and diplomats highly suspect.

The clerics who support Iran's nuclear "menace" also benefit themselves from a fantastically successful money-making operation. In the summer of 2003, *Forbes* magazine featured an article by a senior editor, Paul Klebnikov. The title tells us much: "Iran: The Millionaire Clerics Who Run the Nuclear Menace." The subtitle pulls no punches either: "Millionaire Mullahs: a nuclear threat to the rest of the world, Iran is robbing its own people of prosperity. But the men at the top are getting extremely rich."[85]

---

85. Paul Klebnikov, "Iran," *Forbes*, 6/11/2004, 56-60. The author earned a PhD in Russian History from the London School of Economics and, among other works, wrote *Godfather of the Kremlin, Boris Berezovsky*, which explains how a corrupt, oligarchic capitalist system evolved in Russia. In the summer of 2004, he was shot to death by unknown gunmen in Moscow.

Klebnikov compares the Iranian economy to the "crony capitalism that sprouted from the wreck of the Soviet Union. The 1979 revolution expropriated the assets of foreign investors and the nation's wealthiest families; oil had long been nationalized, but the *mullahs** seized virtually everything else of value—banks, hotels, car and chemical companies, makers of drugs and consumer goods." Rafsanjani, a former president who facilitated the release of Western hostages in Lebanon in the early 1990s, fared well. So did several in his clan. One brother heads Iran's largest copper mine, a brother-in-law became governor of a province, a cousin dominates the pistachio export business, a son and a nephew received key positions in the Ministry of Oil, and another son heads a large Teheran construction project. Other families also benefit from extensive monopolies.

Klebnikov writes, "Dozens of interviews with businessmen, merchants, economists and former ministers and other top government officials reveal a picture of a dictatorship run by a shadow government . . . . Its economy is dominated by shadow business empires." Part of these empires are the Islamic foundations for religious education, theology, or charity, which, according to Klebnikov "account for 10% to 20% of the nation's GDP—$115 billion last year [2003]." Many observers believe this figure rose to 30 percent in 2005. The mission of the foundations, or *bonyads*, is to provide welfare to the people. In theory they are under the Supreme Leader, but in effect they operate without oversight and may serve as slush funds for the clerics who manage them, according to Klebnikov.

Klebnikov continues: "Meanwhile the clerical elite has mismanaged the nation into senseless poverty. . . . per capita income today is actually 7% below what it was before the revolution. Iranian economists estimate capital flight (to Dubai and other safe havens)

---

* A *mullah* is a cleric trained in law and religious doctrine. In other contexts, it can mean teacher.

at up to $3 billion a year." Robbed of their future, Klebnikov explains, "many students turn to the streets in protest."

Commenting on these self-aggrandizing abuses, Ayatollah Taheri, a distinguished senior cleric in Iran, writes, "When I hear that some of the privileged progeny and special people, some of whom even don cloaks and turbans, are competing amongst themselves to amass the most wealth, I am drenched with the sweat of shame."[86]

86. Ibid.

PART TWO

MUSLIM ECONOMIES, PROPERTY OWNERSHIP, AND TERRORISM

CHAPTER 7

MUSLIM ECONOMIES MEASURED BY *INDEX OF ECONOMIC FREEDOM, 2005*

For several years the Heritage Foundation and the *Wall Street Journal* have been co-publishing an *Index of Economic Freedom* for nearly all countries of the world. Each country is rated from 1 (excellent) to 5 (poor) in the following categories: international trade, fiscal burden, government intervention in the economy, monetary policy, foreign investment, banking and finance, government control of wages and prices, property rights, regulation, and informal or black market. A total score is calculated. A low score gives the most positive outlook for prosperity.

The range of scores of Muslim countries from the report:

Economic Freedom	Scores	Countries *
Free	1.00 to 1.99	None
Mostly Free	2.00 to 2.99	Bahrain, Israel, Jordan, Kuwait, Oman, Saudi Arabia, United Arab Emirates
Mostly Unfree	3.00 to 3.99	Algeria, Egypt, Lebanon, Morocco, Qatar, Syria, Tunisia, Turkey, Yemen
Repressed	4.00 to 5.00	Iran, Libya

* Data for Iraq is incomplete.

THE EXAMPLE OF IRAN IN THE *INDEX OF ECONOMIC FREEDOM, 2005*

The following text is paraphrased.

Trade Policy, 2.0. The average tariff rate is moderately low. The main instruments of commercial policy have been non-tariff barriers and the system of multiple exchange rates.

Fiscal Burden of Government, 3.6. The top income tax rate is 35 percent and the top corporate rate is 25 percent. However, government expenditures as a share of Gross Domestic Product increased 5 percent over the previous year.

Government Intervention in the Economy, 5. International Monetary Fund reported that in 2002 the government received 54.24 percent of total revenues from state-owned property and enterprises. This underestimates the level of state involvement. The *Economist* Intelligence Unit (EIU) reports that "inefficient state owned enterprises and politically powerful individuals and institution such as the *bonyad* (Islamic 'charities' that control large business conglomerates) have established a tight grip on much of the non-oil economy utilizing their preferential access" to credit, licenses and public contracts to protect their position. It is difficult for the private sector to compete.

Monetary Policy, 4.0. The average annual rate of inflation was just under 15 percent.

Capital Flows and Foreign Investment, 4.0. The foreign investment code was updated in 2002. According to the *Economist* Intelligence Unit, the code does not permit a market share in one sector by foreign firms of greater than 25 percent or 35 percent in an individual industry, and there is uncertainty in how to apply these rulings. The involved bureaucracy is extensive. The International Monetary fund reports that most payments and transfers face limitations, quantitative limits, or approval requirements. All credit operations face government controls, as do most personal capital movements. (There is latent political hostility towards foreign business in Iran's constitution.)

Banking and Finance, 5.0. Charging interest is restricted under Islamic law. Much of the loans of commercial banks is in low-return loans to state-owned enterprises . . . . Private banks are now allowed and according to the government four are now operating.

Wages and Prices, 4.0. *Economist* Intelligence Unit found that Iran does not regulate pricing of most commercial products with the exception of fuel, and wheat for production of bread. The U.S. Energy Information Administration reports that Iran provides about $3 billion in subsidies for oil. Government also affects prices and wages through extensive state-owned enterprises.

Property Rights, 5.0. These rights are not protected. The rule of law is inconsistent and unsatisfactory. . . The judicial system is opaque and slow-moving, and Iranian parties—both public and private—are adept in delaying tactics. Private investment is permitted in state land but not land ownership.

Regulation, 5.0. The government effectively discourages the establishment of new businesses. The EIU says "Contract negotiations are often lengthy, exhaustive details demanded by state agencies, slow functioning bureaucracy . . . ." Corruption is a continuing problem.

Black Market, 4.0. Smuggling is rampant and includes currency. The informal sector (the underground economy) is very large.

THE LEVEL OF BUSINESS OPPORTUNITIES IN MUSLIM COUNTRIES DERIVED FROM THE *INDEX OF ECONOMIC FREEDOM* BY THE AUTHOR

I find that certain of the categories of the Index—Regulation, Banking and Finance, and Property Rights—are especially significant for measuring the difficulties faced by local people in starting a business, expanding it, and keeping it in existence. The entrepreneur first must go through a regulatory process that may involve contacting several agencies to satisfy many requirements. Perhaps this will involve extremely long waits, months or even years, to learn if approval has been given. Bribes might be expected. If successfully completed, the next likely step is to obtain a bank loan. Is credit available to a new applicant, or do generous loans made to government and its enterprises and well-connected individuals absorb most of the available capital? Can a loan be obtained at market rates? If all is accomplished and the enterprise or expansion comes into existence, will laws enforce contracts and payments due? Do the courts settle disputes fairly and expeditiously? Together, the steps in this long process spell out private business opportunity. ("1" is best; "5" is worst.)

If any of these steps fail or are discouraged at the outset, the business may come into existence as part of the Informal Market (or Black Market), and this becomes a secondary indication of the encouragement or discouragement of business growth.

Business opportunities derived from the *Index*:

Country	Regulation	Banking and Finance	Property Rights	Business Opportunities*	Informal Market
Bahrain	2.0	1.0	1.0	1.33	2.0
Israel	3.0	3.0	2.0	2.67	1.5
Jordan	3.0	2.0	3.0	2.67	3.0
Kuwait	3.0	3.0	3.0	3.00	2.5
Saudi Arabia	3.0	4.0	3.0	3.33	3.0
Turkey	4.0	4.0	3.0	3.67	3.5
Egypt	4.0	4.0	3.0	3.67	3.5
Morocco	3.0	4.0	4.0	3.67	4.0
Algeria	3.0	4.0	4.0	3.67	4.0
Syria	4.0	5.0	4.0	4.33	5.0
Iran	5.0	5.0	5.0	5.00	5.0
Libya	5.0	5.0	5.0	5.00	5.0

Business Opportunities (not an *Index* category) is the average of columns 1, 2, and 3.

CHAPTER 8

A CORRELATION BETWEEN TERRORISM AND OVERWHELMING OWNERSHIP OF PRODUCTIVE PROPERTY BY MUSLIM GOVERNMENTS

The growing influence of Islamic fundamentalism in the last half of the twentieth century and the rise of Islamic terrorism in recent decades have many roots and many sources of nourishment. Understanding has come from scholars, politicians, and journalists, both Muslim and Western. Surely one factor is the placement of the Middle East in the path of the mammoth struggle between Communism and capitalism, especially as it played out in Afghanistan.

Another factor is the immense imbalance between ownership (or direct control) of productive property by governments and ownership by the people. There is a correlation between this imbalance in ownership and terrorism. (Correlation describes the extent certain conditions occur together and does not indicate that one is the cause of the other.)

THE NATIONALIZATION OF INDUSTRY

Most countries in the world of Islam have been a colony of a European nation,* the only exceptions in the Middle East and North Africa being Turkey, Saudi Arabia, and Oman. Turkey emerged from the final decline of the Ottoman Empire as an independent country in 1923. Saudi Arabia, almost ignored by the colonial powers, was always more or less independent. Oman was never a colony but for a long time came under British influence. All the others were swept by waves of nationalism. A few took large steps towards independence beginning in 1922, and all achieved or were given independence in

---

* The colonial powers in the Middle East and North Africa were France, Great Britain, Italy, Spain and Russia. Their merchants and missionaries in the 1800s carried in a counter-force, the idea of political freedom.

the decades after World War II. Finally, the dismemberment of the Soviet Union gave independence to countries in central Asia and between the Caspian and Black Seas.

The nationalization of business enterprises by the newly independent governments was almost inevitable. Since public utilities had been owned by foreign companies, these immediately fell under the control of new governments. This included banks of issue, railroads, telephones, and other public utilities. The beneficiaries were some local businesses, but especially the governments. In addition, when foreigners lost the privileges they had enjoyed, local enterprises became more prosperous and government revenues from taxes grew. Abundant oil deposits were discovered in the region in the first decades of the twentieth century. The expansion of riches in oil in the Middle East and Africa coincided with the rise of nationalism and government control. During the 1950s more lucrative contracts were made with foreign oil companies, and Iran nationalized its oil industry.

Several of these governments decreed land reform in this period. The intention was to improve agriculture and to bring justice to dispossessed people, but this reform actually had the effect of strengthening government. Almost everywhere large landowners were the most powerful class, and they possessed the most capital and were a balance to the economic power of government. The new governments struck a blow at this class, reducing the size of their legal holdings and usually redistributing their land to small farmers. The military government that took power in Egypt in 1952 confiscated large estates, including those of the royal family. The military government moved towards nationalization of the economy, and in 1961 it took over all banks and insurance companies and almost all large industrial companies.* This rendered landowners and commercial interests too weak to challenge their government.

* Later Egyptian governments backed away from this course and began privatizing some government enterprises.

Socialism gave legitimacy to governmental control of large enterprises and property. At this time socialism was enjoying considerable support in countries of Eastern Europe and elsewhere, and Communism also was being energetically promulgated around the world by the Soviet Union. The influence of both grew in Muslim countries. Because the control of productive wealth under socialism and Communism is done in the name of all the people, a responsive chord was struck among pious Muslims. Islamic emphasis on the ideal of social justice prepared people to embrace socialism.

Westerners associate socialism with democracy, but just as often it is associated with military governments. (For instance, the Nazi Party began as a socialist movement.) A government under military officers appeared in Egypt in 1952, and Gamal Abdal Nasser rose to the leadership position. Within a few years Algeria, Libya, Sudan, North Yemen, Syria, and Iraq all fell under military control. Egyptian historian Sameh al-Qaranshawi placed the responsibility for this transformation of governments on the shoulders of Nasser: "Nasser's leadership infected Arab nationalism with the germ of authoritarianism, a crippling disease it has suffered from ever since."[87] These governments continually needed to fortify their power with censorship, secret police, torture, and phony elections.

The military offered both stability and efforts toward economic progress, goals also met and avowed by the monarchical rule of kings and emirs in some Arab countries. The United States and nations of Europe recognized and sometimes supported the undemocratic regimes of the Middle East. The West's reliance on oil from Muslim lands inclined Western nations to support stability—or what they thought would be stability—over change. Domestic groups working for change in some Arab countries became disillusioned with Western democratic governments and resented their interference.

87. "Egypt's 50th anniversary," The Economist, 7/27/2002.

Supporting stability also was part of the struggle between free nations and the worldwide reach of Communism. As Ralph Peters noted, "Overvaluing stability is a heritage of the Cold War, over the course of which we rationalized our support of some very cruel regimes and we deposed elected governments we didn't like. You could justify it in terms of the greater struggle. But you can't justify it now." He concludes, "In the underdeveloped world an obsession with stability means preserving failure and worse."[88]

THE WEALTH OF GOVERNMENTS APPARENTLY INVOLVED IN TERRORISM

Many locations demonstrate the handiwork of terrorists: from Indonesia to Morocco, from the Philippines to Spain, and many other places. But their *governments* have not sponsored these activities, and they do not disengage in opposing terrorism. On the contrary, their laws and administrations work to bring terrorists to justice. The *governments* alleged or proven by Western governments to have materially supported terrorism, or stood by passively, are Libya, Iraq, Iran, Saudi Arabia, Syria, Yemen, and Algeria. All except Syria and Yemen produce considerable amounts of oil and other petroleum products, own large oil fields, and even in some cases, own the petroleum industry. The percentage of income each government derives from its ownership of various enterprises and property is as follows: Syria, 40 percent; Iran, 54 percent; Algeria, 65 percent; Yemen, 70 percent; Saudi Arabia, 78 percent; Libya, over 78 percent.

In Iraq rich oil reserves are owned by the government, although oil production has dropped due to neglect of the fields and to sabotage after a coalition of forces led by the United States entered the country in 2003.

88. Ralph Peters, an interview with F. Smoler, *American Heritage*, March 2003.

A burgeoning portion of government wealth in these countries is in natural resources, either petroleum or phosphate. By 1960 the percentages of government revenue from the petroleum industry were 61 percent in Iraq, 81 percent in Saudi Arabia, and almost 100 percent in certain of the small Gulf States. Iran had nationalized the oil industry. In Syria, 25 percent of revenue came from pipelines running through its territory. Tunisia took over its phosphates industry, and Jordan invested heavily in phosphates, but these resources do not produce great wealth. Another country with phosphates, Morocco, chose the slower route of private enterprise to develop the deposits and did not nationalize them.

Algeria, Libya, and Syria are under military governments, as was Iraq until Saddam Hussein was removed. Saudi Arabia and Iran are not under military governance, but are implicated in the instigation or support of terrorism. They also happen to possess extremely rich petroleum deposits, and their governments are greatly influenced by religious ideals. The government of Saudi Arabia is inordinately responsive to its Wahhabi clerics, and Iran is virtually controlled by its Shi'a clerics. These two governments espouse extreme Islamic fundamentalism, and each works to export its particular form of religion to other parts of the world. They seem to be in competition with each other. Directly or indirectly, they support acts of terrorism and recruit terrorists.

In terms of world opinion, it costs something for the political leaders of these countries, and their privileged elite, to be linked with terrorism. Why does it seem worthwhile to them? Does the lure of immense wealth owned by government bring forth a parade of rivals for power? Do these leaders live in fear of being overturned by internal revolts on the one hand, and from having to compete with the accomplishments of modern democracy on the other?

Surely these rulers and their privileged circles were alarmed when Muslim groups in some countries began stirring and seeking power, and their fears were exacerbated after 1973 when the price of oil skyrocketed, taking the value of their wealth to new heights. Other price hikes occurred, and then the year 1979 saw a series of events very unsettling to oil-rich governments. Saddam Hussein took the presidency in Iraq, the revolution in Iran unseated the shah, the Soviets invaded Afghanistan, and then came a bloody takeover of the Grand Mosque in Mecca by militants. In the 1980s Iran set up government agencies and funded efforts to spread its form of religion to other countries, and the Saudis began to finance the spread of Wahhabism around the world.* Freedom fighters in Afghanistan were funded by Western nations to stop the march of Communism and by Saudi Arabia to deny expansion to the Soviet Union. Osama bin Laden was sent by Saudi Arabia to enter the fight, and circumstances (and funding) allowed him and others to make *jihad* their life work, terrorism their tool and their product.

Meanwhile, high prices of oil had stimulated conservation of energy around the world, and the price of oil dropped, having begun to slip in 1982. Nevertheless, oil produced great profits. These decades saw the rise of virulent terrorism funded by several Muslim countries, especially Saudi Arabia. "The world's largest oil producer had somehow become, as a senior U.S. Treasury Department official put it, 'the epicenter' of terrorist financing." [89]

What is the economic situation of Muslim countries, particularly those with governments involved in terrorism at some time in the past decade? The *Index of Economic Freedom* offers comparisons. As noted earlier, the *Index* identifies countries as Free, Mostly Free,

---

* Shi'a Islam predominates in Iran. Shi'ites have a different history from the majority Sunni Muslims, and they follow strict rules of purity and avoidance of the unclean. Wahhabism, a fundamentalist variant of the Sunni Muslims, dominates in Saudi Arabia.
89. David E. Kaplan, "How billions in oil money spawned a global terror network," *U.S. News*, 12/15/2003.

Mostly Unfree, and Repressed. Eighteen Muslim countries are listed below. Due to incomplete information, Iraq was not completely evaluated in reports from the late 1990s to the present, but in previous years it was considered Repressed. It is omitted below.

Scores for 18 countries on *Index of Economic Freedom, 2005*:

(1 is best, 5 is worst) *

MOSTLY FREE (2.00 to 2.99)		MOSTLY UNFREE and REPRESSED (3.00 to 5.00)	
Bahrain	2.10	Lebanon	3.05
Israel	2.36	Qatar	3.10
United Arab Emirates (UAE)	2.68	Tunisia	3.14
Kuwait	2.76	Morocco	3.18
Jordan	2.79	Egypt	3.38
Oman	2.81	Turkey	3.46
Saudi Arabia	2.99	**Algeria**	**3.49**
		Yemen	**3.70**
		Syria	**3.88**
		Iran	**4.16**
		Libya	**4.40**

* Countries notable for involvement in terrorism are in **bold print** and have the highest scores.

WHO OWNS PROPERTY IN A COUNTRY INVOLVED IN TERRORISM?

Three features stand out among the property-ownership customs that are characteristic of countries involved in terrorism:

(1) overwhelming government ownership of productive enterprises

(2) low levels of private ownership

(3) many obstacles in the way of wealth creation by individuals and private companies, whether domestic or foreign

The *Index of Economic Freedom* evaluates countries on their "government intervention in the economy" on a scale of 1 (good, limited) to 5 (poor, extensive) based on the percentages of government revenue obtained from government-owned enterprises, level of government consumption of the country's domestic product, and, where it occurs, economic favoritism. Nearly always intervention is extremely high for countries involved in terrorism.

The following table gives the percentages of government income derived from government property and also the *Index* ratings of each country on Government Intervention, Regulation, Banking and Finance, and Property Rights. I also include ratings for the Informal Market, because when standard legal, political, and economic processes are slow and arbitrary, some applicants give up and may operate in the informal, black-market economy. Unemployment, a danger signal for involvement in terrorism, also appears in the table. The table entries are sorted according to Percentage of Revenue from Government Ownership.

Government property and private property:

(Countries active in terrorism are in **bold print**)
Data in columns 1 through 6 is taken from the *Index of Economic Freedom, 2005*. Unemployment data
(most are estimates for 2004) is from *CIA World Fact Book*.

Country	% of Govt revenue from govt-owned property and business	Govt intervention in the economy	Regula-tion	Banking and Finance	Private property rights	Informal Market	% of Unem-ployment
Morocco	4.5	2.5	3	4	4	3.5	12.1
Israel	2.9	2.5	3	3	2	2.0	10.7
Turkey	6.6	2.5	4	4	3	3.5	9.3
Jordan	7.6	3.0	3	2	3	3.0	15-30
Tunisia	8.8	2.5	3	4	3	3.0	13.8
Egypt	12.0	3.0	4	4	3	3.5	10.9
Lebanon	18.8	3.0	4	2	4	4.0	18.0
Syria	40.0	4.5	4	5	4	3.5	20.0
Iran	54.3	4.5	5	5	5	3.5	11.2
Bahrain	59.3	4.5	2	1	1	2.5	15.0
United Arab Emirates (UAE)	64.5	2.0	3	4	3	2.5	2.4
Qatar	64.7	4.5	4	3	3	2.5	2.7
Algeria	65.2	4.0	3	4	4	4.0	25.4
Yemen	70.0	4.0	4	4	3	4.0	35.0
Oman	73.2	4.5	3	3	3	2.0	15.0
Saudi Arabia	77.8	4.5	3	4	3	3.0	25.0
Libya	78.0	4.0	5	5	5	4.0	30.0
Kuwait	88.4	4.5	3	3	3	2.5	2.2

AN ECONOMIC PROFILE FOR TERRORISM?

The governments of Syria, Iran, Algeria, Yemen, and Libya—countries apparently involved in terrorism—obtain a large amount of revenue from owning productive property. In the case of Syria, that ownership is not outright, but government control of productive property is overwhelming. The economy of Syria is called a "statist economy." These governments also have poor *Index* ratings in Government Intervention, Regulation, Banking and Finance, Property Rights, and Informal Market. Unemployment is very high. Saudi Arabia rates very poorly in government intervention in the economy and has middling ratings in three of the four areas that relate to private property, hence its "profile" is only borderline. Yet Saudi religious foundations and perhaps the Saudi government are well known as sources of terrorist financing. Despite immense income from petroleum, the countries of Algeria, Iran, Libya, and Saudi Arabia—four of the six "prime suspects"—do not generate enough jobs to overcome high unemployment. In Iran many of the jobs are with government entities.

Lebanon has a number of poor scores and a rating of 3 for Government Intervention. Any encouragement of terrorism by its government is obscured by the heavy hand of Syria in the country, and by the presence of a Hezbollah army in the south. Morocco has several unfavorable scores, and Moroccan individuals have been active in terrorism, notably in attacks on commuter trains in Madrid. But the Moroccan *government* has not been involved.

The small Gulf States have a huge proportion of government revenue coming from government-owned property, yet they are not involved in terrorism. This seeming contradiction will be discussed below. First, let's look at governments with little property.

GOVERNMENTS OWNING LITTLE PRODUCTIVE PROPERTY HAVE NOT BEEN INVOLVED IN TERRORISM

This section draws on tables 5 and 6 above. Jordan does not appear on the above list of terrorist countries. Rather, Jordan ranks as Mostly Free and gets little revenue from government-held property. The property that it does hold consists mostly of large phosphate deposits.

Egypt, Morocco, Tunisia, and Turkey rank as Mostly Unfree, but receive little revenue from government-held property. Egypt receives 12 percent; the others from 4 to 9 percent. Egypt does have petroleum deposits, but this wealth is balanced by a large agriculture base and production in textiles and aluminum, most under private ownership. With coercion and vigilance, the Egyptian government has generally been able to control extremist Islamic parties within its borders. In Turkey, even though the 2002 election in Turkey was won by an Islamic Party, the new administration has elements of moderation. Turkey actually imports oil. Tunisia and Morocco have phosphate resources, but little or no petroleum. King Mohammad VI of Morocco has his authorities work against Islamic extremism. One initiative is the placement in mosques of wide-screen televisions broadcasting a moderate version of Islam.

EXCEPTIONS TO THE CORRELATION OF GOVERNMENT OWNERSHIP AND TERRORISM

The countries of Kuwait, Bahrain, the United Arab Emirates, Qatar, and Oman also do not appear on the list of terror-supporting states. With the exception of Oman, all are territorially small. All, including Oman, export oil and are ruled by kings, emirs, or sultans. These countries derive from 59 to 88 percent of revenue from government-owned property. This seems to be evidence counter to the proposition that terrorism is associated with extensive government ownership of productive property. Perhaps these countries are exceptions to the rule because governments do not impose prohibitively heavy burdens on businesses owned or being created by individuals.

Business opportunities in small Gulf states:

Country	Regulation	Banking and Finance	Property Rights	Business Opportu- nities	Informal Market
Bahrain	2	1	1	1.33	2.0
Kuwait	3	3	3	3.00	2.5
Oman	3	3	3	3.00	2.0
United Arab Emirates (UAE)	3	4	3	3.33	2.5
Qatar	4	3	3	3.33	2.5
Syria	4	5	4	4.33	5.0

Syria is included for contrast.

Located on ancient sea routes, these small countries of the Persian Gulf have long been influenced by their merchant communities. They have had close contact with Great Britain and are influenced by common law. Bahrain, Kuwait, Oman, and the UAE give good to moderate protection to private property and are rated by the *Index of Economic Freedom, 2005*, as Mostly Free. Qatar, on the other hand, is Mostly Unfree, and has occasionally been accused of terrorist contacts, but it has not been deeply involved in terrorist activities.

The following paragraphs describe "Business Opportunities," a category derived from the *Index of Economic Freedom, 2005* for the small Gulf countries. These opportunities entice more enterprises into the legal market and less into the informal, black market. In these countries the scores for Informal Market range from 2 to 2.5.

In 2002, Sheikh al-Khalifa of Bahrain willingly gave up his status as absolute monarch, and a referendum approved a constitutional monarchy with an independent judiciary. Women have been given the vote, and property is secure. A total of 74 percent of government income comes from government-owned enterprises and property, much of it petroleum related. However, it is dependent on Saudi Arabia for oil granted as aid.

Kuwait is a constitutional emirate ruled by a parliament and an emir. It is a very large oil producer. Nearly all production is owned by the government. It is a welfare state with the government employing about 95 percent of the workforce. It has a five-year plan to encourage privatization, but people cling to the generous government subsidies. Property is protected, although the legal system is slow.

Oman is a small producer of oil but this sector accounts for most of the government revenues. It has had a series of five-year plans to diversify the economy and facilitate privatization and private employment. It has been friendly to foreign investment.

The United Arab Emirates, made up of seven small kingdoms, was given independence by Great Britain in 1971 and has a constitution that guarantees religious freedom. The legal system centers on Islamic law, but incorporates elements of Western legal systems, especially in commercial law. UAE receives most of its revenues from government-owned petroleum enterprises. It has a generous welfare system, and most of its labor force comes from other Muslim countries. It is an extremely active re-export center with Dubai, a city state, at the center of this activity. Dubai has diversified its economy, welcomed foreign investment, and enjoys an incredibly active economy. It has begun constructing islands on which will be truly fabulous buildings for business and tourism. Abu Dhabi,

UAE's most populous emirate, is an oil producer, and it gives a large part of its wealth to the poorer emirates. Another emirate, Sharjah, has three busy ports. It supports local entrepreneurship and has a Chamber of Commerce of 30,000 members. Its Sheikh, Dr. Sultan bin Mohamad Al-Oasimi, wants peace, hosts 1,000 cultural events each year, and promotes exhibitions, tourism, arts, education, etc.

In Qatar, women have the right to vote, and a new constitution grants freedom of the press and religion. Like the other Gulf kingdoms, the government has a number of monopolies. The oil industry is fairly large. Property and contracts are generally secured, although the legal process is long and bureaucratic.

The many examples given in this chapter demonstrate that there is a correlation between high percentages of ownership of productive property by governments and terrorism linked to such countries. Correlation is a measure of the extent certain conditions occur together and does not indicate that one is the cause of the other. However, one may be the necessary condition for the other to exist.

CHAPTER 9

MORE ON ECONOMIC DOMINANCE OF GOVERNMENT AND TERRORISM

This chapter describes economic conditions and characteristics of seven Muslim countries—Algeria, Iran, Iraq, Libya, Saudi Arabia, Syria, and Yemen—and their involvement in terrorism.

ALGERIA

Dominance of the Algerian Government in the Economy

In 2001 the country Algeria received over 60 percent of its total revenues from state-owned enterprises in the hydrocarbon sector where it owns a monopoly. Banking is dominated by six state-owned banks, accounting for up to 95 percent of deposits and assets. Banks continue to finance loss-making enterprises for government, and to lend to cronies of the regime. [90]

Recent Events

Algeria has executed many of its own citizens and has given shelter to terrorists from other countries. Citizens of this country have been involved in terrorist activities in Europe and in America. In 1995 a series of bombings killed seven people in Paris and Lyon. The Armed Islamic Group, a homegrown Algerian group, claimed responsibility, saying they opposed French help being given to the Algerian military regime. Another action was the explosion in a crowded commuter train that killed 4 and wounded 100 in 1996. The arrest of Algerian Ahmed Rassam in Washington, D.C. foiled a plot to attack the U.S. during millennium celebrations. He later testified that he was working under bin Laden's chief of operations. In 2003 seven North Africans, mostly Algerian, were arrested in Britain in connection with possession of the deadly toxin ricin.

90. Heritage Foundation, *Index of Economic Freedom, 2002*, "Algeria."

Intelligence officials in the United States believe Algerian nationals represent the third-largest pool of recruits for al Qaeda, behind Saudi Arabia and Yemen. It is believed that 2,800 Algerians trained at the al Qaeda camps in Afghanistan in recent years. Now, ominously, a new training ground has developed in the desolate regions of southern Algeria that border Mali, Mauritania, Niger, and Chad.

In 1954 Algeria, a colony of France for over a century, began fighting for its independence. After 100,000 French casualties, a million Algerian casualties, and nearly two million refugees, French General Charles de Gaulle declared the war un-winnable in 1961. A democratic socialist state was then organized under the direction of the Algerian army. A fundamentalist political party emerged in the 1980s and made a very good showing in the election of 1992. (This portended an Islamic dictatorship, and demonstrated a weakness of democracy if it is only a voting process unsupported by an economically strong middle class. This was expressed as: "One man, one vote, *one time.*") Thereupon, a group of military and civilian officials annulled the election, and a bloody insurgency began. Four years later a constitutional amendment effectively banned political parties based on religion or on ethnicity. Internal troubles have subsided but there is discontent over crumbling infrastructure and joblessness.

IRAN

Dominance of the Iranian Government in the Economy The Iranian oil industry, its largest industry, was nationalized under the Shah in the 1950s, and this is the country's leading industry. The top income tax rate is 54 percent and the top corporate tax rate has been reduced to 25 percent. However, inefficient state-owned enterprises and Islamic charities control large business conglomerates, and these have preferential access to credit, licenses, and public contracts, all of which make it difficult for private businesses to compete. Protection of property rights is weak. Government economic power is demonstrated by massive subsidies that keep prices low, especially for fuel, power, and food. Before the 2006 increase in the price of oil, gasoline was 10 percent of its international price. The country carries a heavy load of international debt and must import gasoline since its refinery capacity is inadequate. It imports 40 percent of its gasoline mostly from France, India, Turkey, and the Gulf states.[91]

Recent Events

Recently the Revolutionary Guard, the elite military, has been gaining power inside the Iranian government. It worked quietly for two years for the election of President Mahmoud Ahmadinejad. According to experts, "The Guard is a veritable state within the state: it has its own intelligence agency and prisons, three universities . . . . and its own think tanks. It even has its own ports of entry."[92] It operates companies that won multibillion-dollar contracts for an oil pipeline and for a subway. Six billion dollars in oil revenue may have disappeared from their accounts.

Since his election, Ahmadinejad has begun to enrich uranium— for peaceful purposes he claims. Iran, however, possesses long-range missiles that can carry nuclear weapons. The president has solidified his power with the public by raising salaries for workers in the vast, government-controlled industrial sector and also for everyone else. He doubled grants for newlyweds and caused interest rates to be lowered. The previous market-based approach has been reversed. Unemployment remains high as hundreds of thousands of young people flood the labor market each year, and the new policies may

91. Heritage Foundation, op. cit. 2005, "Iran."
92. Abbas Milani and Michael McFaul (both of Stanford University), "Negotiate, But Support Iran's Democrats," *St. Paul Pioneer Press*, 6/25/2006.

push inflation, already at 15 percent, even higher.[93] The middle class is under stress, and more and more people hold two jobs.

In 1979 a revolution in Iran unseated the Shah, and students in Teheran lost no time in stoning the U.S. Embassy and taking hostages on November 4, 1979. Concurrently, Iran demanded an apology from the United States for supporting the Shah and the return of money they said he had hoarded in the U.S. The International Court of Justice ordered the return of hostages but Iran ignored the order. In the spring Americans staged a commando raid which failed tragically. Iranian assets in the U.S. were frozen. At length, after the United States agreed to return the Iranian assets and pledged non-interference in their affairs, the 53 Americans were freed. They had been held 444 days.

Sometime after the revolution had succeeded Ayatollah Ruhollah Khomeini seized control and established something like a "theocracy." The leaders of the new Islamic Republic felt they could not survive without spreading their system to other countries. They looked at the arguments of Communist leader Leon Trotsky for "a permanent world revolution." He had said that when the proletarian revolution is confined to one country it will suffocate; to thrive it must expand to other countries. When the spread of Communism was stopped around the world the Soviet Union did indeed collapse, and this was taken as a warning of what could happen to Iranian "theocracy" if it failed to expand.[94]

The prime minister in the early years, Mir-Hussein Moussavi, said, "Immediately after the revolution, we had our own vision of 'exporting revolution,' believing that the Islamic revolution would spread in the region within one year in a chain reaction. It seems,

93. BILL SPINDLE, "Behind Rise of Iran's President, A Populist Economic Agenda," *Wall Street Journal,* 6/22/2006.
94. MOHAMMAD MOHADDESSIN, *Islamic Fundamentalism,* 1993, 36. Citation from newspaper *Ressalat,* July 7, 1991.

however, that we were mistaken." They learned that to achieve their objectives they must create a government organization to promote that goal.[95] Therefore, in 1990 the Quds Force was established, the most secret of the regime's numerous military organizations. It coordinates all terrorist acts. Its General Staff for Export of Revolution oversees separate Directorates for various locations:

1. Iraq

2. Palestine, Lebanon, Jordan

3. Turkey

4. Afghanistan, Pakistan, India

5. Europe and the United States

6. North Africa

7. Arabian Peninsula

8. Republics of the former Soviet Union

As a first step in exporting the "Islamic Revolution," the Shi'ite regime aimed religious propaganda toward neighboring Iraq where the Shi'ites were about 60 percent of the population. This was a threat to the rule of Saddam Hussein, and that irritation, in addition to a border dispute, brought the two countries to war by 1980. After two years Hussein offered peace because the war was going staggeringly poorly for the Iraqis, but Iranian leaders wanted public support at home and so stoked the war fires for several more years. Iran would likely have defeated Iraq had the United States not provided significant support to Iraq, including arms and intelligence such as satellite images detailing likely sites of Iranian attacks.[96] Defeat of Iran came in 1988 after a million Iranians were killed, hundreds of thousand being children in the front lines or sacrificed in clearing mine fields.*

95. Ibid., 98, 100.
96. Kurt Burch, "Iran-Iraq War," *Encyclopedia of the Twentieth Century*, Pasadena, CA: Salem Press, 2007.
* Khomeini was asked, "For a child to serve is parental consent necessary?" His answer was, "So long as there is military need, serving is a religious duty and parental consent is not necessary." Khomeini gave permission to kill enemy civilians and prisoners of war. From Mohaddessin, op.cit., 62.

The revolution in Iran, a heavily Shi'ite country, and its expansionist ambitions were unsettling to the governments of countries with Shi'ite minorities: Kuwait, Syria, Lebanon, and Saudi Arabia. There were intrusive activities by Iran into Jordan, Lebanon, Algeria, Tunisia, Sudan, Morocco, Saudi Arabia, the Persian Gulf States, and Egypt, causing the latter to break diplomatic relations with Iran. Expansionist activity, seen in 1985 in Madrid when a bomb killed 18 and injured 82, was claimed by Shi'ite extremists.

After the fall of Saddam Hussein in 2003, the United States accused the Quds Force of arming Iraqi militants with deadly bombs. According to news reports, "Experts said the specialized and highly secretive Commando units were sent abroad to assist fellow Shi'ites usurp monarchies in the Persian Gulf and gun down enemies abroad and Israelis forces in southern Lebanon."[97]

The militant armed group, Hezbollah, was formed by Iran. It entered into Lebanon to oppose Israel's occupation of the buffer "zone" in the south of Lebanon separating Israeli territory and Arab territory. In Lebanon Hezbollah is supported by both Iran and Syria. In the 1980s this group kidnapped 30 Western hostages in Lebanon, and some were executed. The first use of suicide bombing was carried out by Hezbollah against the U.S. embassy in Beirut in April 1983. Seven months later a suicide member of this group drove a truck into the barracks in Beirut that killed 241 Marines and nearly 80 French soldiers. Hezbollah members hijacked a TWA airplane and executed a U.S. Navy man. In 1994 Hezbollah bombed a Jewish center in Buenos Aires, killing 85 people, and in 1996 truck-bombed Khobar Towers in Saudi Arabia, killing 19 American servicemen. It has been said that this group has killed more Americans than any other except al-Qaeda.

97. News services, "Iran's Quds Force is dangerous, deadly," *St. Paul Pioneer Press*, 2/16/2007.

When Israel vacated southern Lebanon, Hezbollah fortified the area working with Iranian Revolutionary Guards in a planning and designing capacity. Most of Hezbollah's weapons have come from Iran and Syria. In the summer of 2006 it took two Israeli soldiers hostage, and Israel invaded Lebanon in a short, indecisive war.

Hezbollah is well funded. The United States government has blacklisted more than 400 entities worldwide for allegedly giving material support to terrorist groups, and about a dozen apparently have links to Hezbollah. The U.S. government has successfully prosecuted two men for running a cigarette smuggling ring that funnels money to Hezbollah, and has frozen the assets of Al-Manar satellite TV channel and the Nour radio channel in the U.S., both owned by Lebanese. The broadcast organizations are accused of recruiting soldiers and sending money to the group. Government officials also have arrested nine men in Detroit for raising funds for Hezbollah.[98] Anti-terrorism experts think that Hezbollah will not stage attacks in the United States because this country is a source of so much of its funding.

On the weekend of June 26, 2004, U.S. authorities expelled two security guards at the Iranian mission to the United Nations after the mission was warned repeatedly against permitting its employees to videotape the Statue of Liberty, the subway, bridges, and other New York landmarks. "What's Iran Up To?" asks an editorial writer in the *Wall Street Journal*. He asks the reader to consider a statement made two weeks earlier in Teheran by one Hannan Abbassi, head of the government's Revolutionary Guards' Center for Doctrinaire Affairs of National Security Outside Iran's Borders: "We will map 29 sensitive sites in the United States and give the information to all international terror organizations." Days later Mr. Abassi was reported saying, "We have a strategy drawn up for the destruction of Anglo-Saxon civilization."[99]

98. Jay Solomon, "U.S. Targets Hezbollah Funds," *Wall Street Journal*, 4/24/2006.
99. *Wall Street Journal*, editorial, 7/1/2004.

IRAQ

Dominance of the Iraqi Government in the Economy*

Between 1972 and 1975, oil in Iraq was nationalized. In 1973 oil prices skyrocketed, and the government became the primary agent for transferring wealth from oil production and export to the rest of the economy. The Iraqi government was the determiner of employment, income distribution, and development. The government also exerted heavy control over agriculture, trade, communication, banking, public utilities, and industrial production. Most of the large industries had to do with oil. The private sector consisted of small-scale industry, shops, farms, and some services. The agriculture sector was privatized in 1987, but development was hampered by labor shortages, the increasing salinity of some arable land, and dislocations caused by previous land reform and collectivization programs. In the short time since 1987 private ownership of land has not empowered people in this sector, nor is it sufficiently productive. In 1989 it employed about 35 percent of the labor force but accounts for less than 10 percent of the gross national product.

Recent Events

In the Iran-Iraq War, Hussein used poison gas on the battlefield and in 1988 he ordered the use of chemical weapons against 5,000 Iraqi Kurds. In the 1991 Gulf War, Scud-type missiles were fired from Iraq towards Tel Aviv, Israel. Saddam had promised that he would torch Tel Aviv and also sack the pro-American regimes in the Persian Gulf, then share the loot of oil wealth with the multitudes in Jordan and elsewhere. After American and other forces withdrew from Iraq in 1991, Iraqi Shi'ites rebelled, whereupon sulfuric acid and napalm was dropped on them from Iraq military helicopters.

* Information from news sources. Iraq has not been in the *Index of Economic Freedom* in recent years for lack of reliable data.

In 1993 Iraqis made an assassination attempt on President Bush when he visited Kuwait.

Saddam had supported terrorism in Lebanon and made payments of $25,000 to families of suicide bombers. Abu Abbas, who hijacked the ship Achille Lauro, found sanctuary in Iraq. When he was arrested by American Special Forces in April 2003, it was learned he had an arsenal of weapons in what the Associated Press called an abandoned training camp south of Baghdad. Another terrorist, Abu Musad al-Zarqawi, after operating in Afghanistan, opened the Ansar al-Islam base in northern Iraq. He allied his group with al Qaeda in early 2004 after the coalition led by the United States invaded.

In the war to remove Saddam, documents were obtained that revealed details of his intention to produce weapons of mass destruction if the United Nations sanctions were weakened or lifted. In the years leading up to the invasion of Iraq by the U.S.-led coalition, Saddam refused entry to inspectors, who could have cleared Iraq of active development of weapons of mass destruction (WMDs). It seems that due to the sanctions and the "fly-overs" of Iraqi air space by American and British pilots, Iraq had little or no involvement in WMDs at that time.

Economy Injured by Wars, Sanctions, and Fraud

Threatened by the politico-religious philosophy emanating from the Shiite theocracy of Iran, troops of Saddam Hussein invaded Iran in 1980, a war that lasted until 1988, when the United Nations negotiated a cease-fire. All aspects of the Iraqi economy were devastated. The social and economic infrastructure were squandered or destroyed, and the government printing of money sent inflation out of control. Foreign reserves that had been $35 to $40 billion in the early 1980s were then gone. Educated people fled. The government controlled all radio and TV.

In 1990 Kuwait was pumping what Saddam Hussein regarded as excessive amounts of oil, thereby holding down the price of oil, so Hussein ordered his troops to invade Kuwait. A group of Western powers responded in the "Gulf War," quickly defeating Iraq but not destroying its army. United Nations sanctions were then imposed, which under Saddam's fraudulent administration worsened economic conditions. The real gross domestic product (GDP) fell by 75 percent from 1991 to 1999. There was widespread unemployment, and severe shortages of medicine, animal vaccines, farm machinery, electric generating equipment, and water purification supplies. Diseases and malnutrition rose sharply. The United Nations in 1995 allowed the Oil for Food program to be set up, and the Program began the next year administered by the U.N. Saddam was able to extract billions of dollars for himself and his regime in four ways: 1) smuggling oil out of the country, 2) bringing in substandard medicine, 3) demanding kickbacks from those he dealt with in many countries throughout the world, and 4) not maintaining the oil fields with money allocated for that purpose by the U.N. His actions drew many companies and individuals into this pattern of corruption.

The military invasion by a coalition led by the United States in 2003 unseated Saddam, but has been unable to put down a violent insurgency that has played havoc with the economy. The coalition continues to attempt to install a democracy despite the lack of a strong middle class.

LIBYA

Dominance of the Libyan Government in the Economy[100]

Guided by quasi-Marxist economic theories, Libya is dedicated to the redistribution of wealth. Hence the top income tax rate is 90 percent, while the top corporate rate is 64 percent. The leadership used

---

100. Heritage Foundation, op. cit., "Libya."

oil funds in the 1970s and 1980s to promote its form of government elsewhere, supporting subversion of both Marxism and capitalism. The private sector is very small, thus nearly all government income is derived from government-owned enterprises and property.

Recent Events

This country helped and protected terrorist Abu Nidal. It shipped weapons to the Irish Republican Army and subsidizes terrorists in other nations. It was believed that an attack on a German disco in 1985 that killed 3 people and injured 229 was directed by Libya, but subsequent intelligence concluded the perpetrators were Syrians. The U.S. responded that year by bombing Libyan military sites, terrorist locations, and Qadhafi's residence. On December 21, 1988, a bomb on a Pan American 747 airliner sent it crashing into Lockerbie, Scotland killing 11 in the town and 259 on the airplane. Subsequent intelligence from Libyan defectors indicates that Qadhafi ordered the bombing in retaliation for the U.S. attack. It took Libya nearly 15 years to take responsibility and negotiate compensation. In 1992 Libya was accused of the manufacture of chemical weapons, and the United Nations imposed sanctions for its refusal to extradite two men accused in the bombing of the Pan American plane. U.N. sanctions were lifted in 1999, although not by the United States until 2004 after Qadhafi promised not to support terrorists or to build nuclear weapons. Libya and Germany are now negotiating payment to 163 of the non-American victims of the 1986 attack.

SAUDI ARABIA

Dominance of the Saudi Government in the Economy [101]

In 2001 state-owned oil companies produced just under 80 percent of total Saudi government revenues. Revenues were $46 billion and

101. Ibid., "Saudi Arabia."

expenditures were $56.5 billion. Only about 25 percent of GDP is generated in the private sector. The rise in the price of oil has greatly increased its revenues.

Recent Events

The governing body of this country, the family of Saud, is closely tied to the Wahhabi sect of Sunni Islam. The *imams* preach violence against non-Wahhabi Muslims and all other faiths. Their fundamentalism is inflexible even though they state that their strict form of Islamic law can evolve cautiously. A measure of inflexibility is demonstrated in the acts of the Religious Police in March 2002, which prevented a rescue of girls in a fire at the Thirty-first Girls' Middle School in Mecca because the girls were not properly dressed. Fourteen died, 50 were injured, and those who escaped on their own soon died.

Although the Saudi rulers were always close to the Wahhabi clerics, three shocks in 1979—the clerical revolution in Iran, the bloody occupation of the Grand Mosque in Mecca, and the Soviets moving into Afghanistan—brought the rulers even closer to the clerics. It was not long before the Saudi family began building immense, grand mosques and large schools to bind the Wahhabi clerics to them. The rulers also began to facilitate the world-wide expansion of the Wahhabi cult, collecting the *zakat* (a traditional tax for charity) for expansion in 1979 and continuing thereafter. Unknown to—or ignored by—leaders in America, Saudi financing of the preaching of Wahhabism around the world is intertwined with inclining young students towards terrorism.

By the late 1980s, quasi-official Islamic charities in Saudi Arabia had become the primary source of funds for the *jihad* movement. The money was used to recruit new members, run paramilitary training camps, and purchase weapons. The goal of the charities was to spread Wahhabism, a fundamentalist sect of Sunni Islam, across the world.

According to an independent agency, the Center for Security Policy, from 1975 through 2002 more than $70 *billion* was spent on overseas aid by the charities. This was money that came from, or through, the Saudi government. A prodigious amount went to build 1,500 mosques, 210 Islamic centers, 202 colleges, and nearly 2,000 schools in non-Islamic countries (including the United States), all promoting the intolerant Wahhabi sect. Alex Alexiev of the CPC calls this "the largest worldwide propaganda campaign ever mounted"—dwarfing the former Soviets' efforts to spread their economic gospel. A blizzard of extremist Wahhabist literature was spread around the world, unsettling moderate Islamic clerics in other countries. [102]

Bernard Lewis illustrates the importance of the educational activities of Saudi Arabia in Muslim countries, Europe and the United States: "Imagine that the Ku Klux Klan. . . obtains control of the state of Texas and its oil and uses this money to establish a network of well-endowed schools and colleges all over Christendom, peddling their peculiar brand of Christianity." [103] Lewis points out that the actual effect of Saudi-financed schools in Muslim countries is more ominous than the Klan scenario because there are no functioning public school systems in those countries. In many places, schools of fundamentalism have a monopoly over education.

When Russia was withdrawing its forces from Afghanistan, the ultra-conservative Taliban (an Afghan tribal-based tradition with extreme repressive customs) advanced into power, and as many as 10,000 Saudis were sent from Arabia to serve with the Taliban forces. One was Osama bin Laden, who created al Qaeda while engaged in this fight. When this war ended he brought terror to other places. The Saudi government has not cooperated with the efforts of other countries to fight terror. Among the many acts of terror of al Qaeda was the 1993 truck bombing of the World Trade Center, and in 1996

102. David E. Kaplan, "Saudi Connection," *U.S. News & World Report*, 12/15/2003, 18–32.
103. Bernard Lewis, *The Crisis of Islam, Holy War and Unholy Terrorism*, 2003, 129.

the Saudi rulers refused the request of the United States to hand over the foremost suspect in that crime. A decade-long investigation of the bombing of the barracks in Lebanon that killed U.S. Marines and French soldiers had led by 1995 to Imad Mughniyah, and he was given protection by the Saudi government. The Saudi government also stymied the FBI investigation of the 1996 Khobar Towers bombing.

"A report submitted to the U.N. secretary-general by an independent consultant on terrorism financing shows that over the last decade Saudi religious charities have channeled up to $500 million to terrorist groups including al Qaeda and Hamas, the latter operating in Israel and taking control of Gaza in 2007. Terrorism needs capital, and it can spread misery fairly cheaply: the 9/11 operations cost al Qaeda approximately one-half million dollars to conduct. Since then, approximately $134 million in terrorist money has been identified and frozen world-wide—a fraction of the total amount available to finance such attacks."[104]

In October 2001, just after the attacks on New York City and Washington, eighty countries were participating in an international consortium that agreed to block assets of terrorist groups, but Saudi Arabia declined to participate! Yet the American government did not express disapproval. "The U.S. is so fearful of 'instability' that it's afraid to criticize the current regime, much less encourage it to move in a more democratic direction . . ."[105]

Stephen Schwartz, author of *The Two Faces of Islam*, says that the facts about Saudi funding of Wahhabism and terrorism are known, and now we need to know how the United States intends to proceed with this problem. He is concerned with American inaction in regard to Saudi funding, and he is concerned with extremist Wahhabi literature that is given to men in prisons in the United States and in the armed forces.

104. Peter Brookes, "Saudis Are Paying the Price for Appeasing Terrorists," *Pioneer Press*, 5/26/2003.
105. Lead editorial, *Wall Street Journal*, 10/30/2001.

The Saudi royal family watched for many years as activities facilitated by money from their country fomented terror elsewhere, and then the homeland itself was attacked! In May and November of 2003, massive attacks in Saudi residential areas killed 72 people. In March 2004, suicide bombers in the capital city of Riyadh killed 6 and injured 148. An attack in Jiddah was foiled in May 2004, but serious attacks occurred afterwards.

"Liberal Saudis have accused the country's religious establishment of laying the groundwork for a long siege with the extremists by inspiring countless frustrated youths to take up arms for *jihad* abroad."[106] Despite pressure from inside the country and outside, it remains to be seen whether Saudi Arabia will shut off the money stream to terrorist organizations.

Meanwhile, terrorists have found other ways to finance acts of destruction. The attacks of March 11, 2004 in Madrid are believed by Spanish authorities to have been funded by the exchange of illicit drugs for explosives. In Europe terrorist organizations engage in smuggling Muslims into various countries, and use the funds they earn to support other activities. Ironically, they use the desire of Muslims to improve their lives by emigrating to Europe to finance terror operations against Europe.

SYRIA

Dominance of the Syrian Government in the Economy[107]

Syria receives around 24 percent of its revenues from state-owned enterprises and property, and a considerable portion of this is from the petroleum industry, particularly pipelines crossing its country. The government also controls port operation, telecommunications, air transport, power and water, and owns the major banks, which

106. Neil MacFarquhar, "Saudi Blast Kills at Least Four," *New York Times*, 4/21/2003.
107. Heritage Foundation, op. cit., "Syria."

tend to lend only to the public sector. Essentially the economy is run by the state.

Recent Events

The involvement of this country in terrorism comes through its encouragement of various anti-Israeli groups, particularly Hezbollah, an organization that is the creation of Iran. Although Syrian Muslims are largely Sunni, the ruling elite, the Alawites, are a Shi'ite minority, and they enjoy a close relationship with Iran where Shi'ite power is centered. Syria, as well as Iran, give support to Hezbollah, also to Hamas.

The former group was responsible for kidnapping several Europeans and Americans in the 1980s, for the 1983 suicide truck bombing in Beirut that killed nearly 300 American and French soldiers, for hijacking TWA flight 847 in 1985, for the bombing of the Israeli embassy in Argentina in 1992 that killed 29 people, and for the bombing of the Argentine Jewish community center in 1994 killing 95 people.

In 1986 the United Kingdom broke diplomatic relations with Syria, and the United States imposed sanctions, both accusing it of sponsoring international terrorism. Again in May 2003, the U.S. imposed economic sanctions on Syria for not doing enough to prevent militants from entering Iraq and for supporting the insurgency against the new Iraqi government. President Bashar Assad said he would not expel militant groups because they were fighting Israel. Currently Assad permits officials of the Palestinian group called Hamas,* identified as a terrorist group, to reside in Damascus.

SYRIA AND LEBANON

Until recently Syrians used Lebanon as a buffer state between themselves and Israel. This situation combined with other stresses to

---

* In January 2006 in an election in Palestine encouraged by the United States, Hammas won a greater number of seats than the Palestinian Liberation Organization.

bring turmoil to Lebanon, which descended into a devastating civil war from 1975 to 1990. Lebanon had become independent after World War II and had prospered under a free-market economy, and because of strict laws on secrecy in banking it became the banking center of the Middle East much as Switzerland is the banking center of Europe. Unfortunately, the Civil War destroyed Lebanon's infrastructure to the extent of 25 to 30 billion dollars, business moved elsewhere, and many Christians departed. Early in the Civil War, Syria invaded Lebanon and became mired in the conflict. Despite a treaty of friendship with Lebanon in 1990, many Syrian troops remained to enforce the will of the Syrian government.

Hezbollah, funded by Iran and encouraged by Syria, has put down roots in southern Lebanon. It has a large network that efficiently delivers social services. With this reservoir of goodwill, Hezbollah sponsored over twenty men who successfully ran for Parliament after Syria withdrew its troops from the country in 2005.[108] In July 2006 its soldiers killed several Israeli soldiers and kidnapped two, an incident that almost immediately flared into war across the Israel-Lebanon border. Hostilities ended after about a month of indecisive fighting, which seems to have increased the influence of Hezbollah in both Lebanon and the Middle East.

In February of 2005 the former Lebanese prime-minister Rafik Hariri was assassinated. What was reported as a purely political event seems now to have had deep economic undercurrents. Michel Prothero writes in the May 15, 2006 issue of *Fortune* that the assassination may have been linked to the collapse of Lebanon's bank al-Medina. The bank's collapse was due to corruption, fraud, and to involvement in Iraq's "Oil for Food" program. The bank was converting hot money into legitimate bank accounts around the world.

108. Karby Leggett, "Mideast Democracy: One Violent Group Finds It Works Fine," *Wall Street Journal*, 7/10/2006.

The United Nations has begun to investigate the assassination of Hariri. Other important Lebanese leaders who are anti-Syrian have been killed or injured. This includes journalist Samir Kassir, politician George Hawi, Defense Minister Elias Murr, who survived bombing, TV announcer May Chidiac, who lost a leg and an arm, editor and publisher Gibran Tueni, and Lebanese Minister Pierre Gemayel. Perhaps the June 2007 bombing in Lebanon that killed another anti-Syrian politician and several of his associates is the response of Syria to the findings of the United Nations.

YEMEN

Dominance of the Yemen Government in the Economy[109]

Seventy percent of Yemen's revenues are from state-owned enterprises and property. Enforcement of contracts is weak, and cases claiming interest payments usually are rejected because of Islamic law. Investment laws are sound but the bureaucracy is inefficient and corrupt.

Recent Events

This small country just to the south of Saudi Arabia provided the second greatest number of fighters for the Afghan war against the Soviet Union. After the war, soldiers were welcomed back, and a few years later they were sent against the Soviet-backed socialists of what was then South Yemen, soon to be united with the north. The present Yemeni government does not act against terrorists. It integrates the Islamists politically rather than suppressing them. In early 2002, extremists held 64 of the 301 seats in parliament and had penetrated the intelligence service, the army, and other departments.[110]

109. Heritage Foundation, op. cit., "Yemen."
110. *The Economist*, "Could Yemen's Calm Be Threatened?," 2/16/2002.

In 2002 a hole was blown in the side of the USS Cole, killing 17 American seamen as she sat in a harbor. In November 2002, the United States, having determined that this was the work of al Qaeda, killed a chief of the organization using a drone that struck his car with a missile. Other plotters were captured, tried, and imprisoned in Yemen. However, in February of 2006 these men escaped through a long tunnel and have disappeared, probably with governmental help.

PART THREE

MUSLIMS TRANSFIXED BY THE GLORY DAYS OF ISLAM

AND

WAYS OUT OF THE ECONOMIC TRAP

CHAPTER 10

FINDING THE WELLSPRING OF BOTH MILITARY SLAVERY AND MODERN TERRORISM

In his unusual book, *Slave Soldiers and Islam: The Genesis of a Military System*, Daniel Pipes traces the development and use of military slavery in Islam. The military divisions he describes were made up of young men from the frontiers. They had been captured as boys, converted to Islam, and were rigorously educated or trained for five years or longer. Since the Qur'an and *shari'a* both guarantee the human dignity of the slave, especially if Muslim, military slaves in Islam were respected and sometimes rose to positions of power. This system was entirely unique to Islam, although slaves serving as soldiers had occurred in various parts of the world, including China, Russia, and the United States during the Civil War. In a highly organized form, and on a large scale, military slavery first appeared in Islam in the ninth century and lasted into the nineteenth century.

Of comparable uniqueness to the Islamic world is the recent outbreak of terrorism connected with extreme Islamic fundamentalism, its anger focused not only on the United States, but also on people connected in any way with Western civilization.

Is it possible that a common thread runs through these two unusual developments? Is there something in the history of Muslims, or in their world view, or even in their theology, that could bring to light an affinity between these two developments—even though they originated in different centuries? There may be.

Muslims throughout their history have embraced as an ideal model the initial social-political life of the seventh century. This vision depicts a unified Muslim community, or *umma*, that fought only against infidels and a form of "just rule" in which caliphs were selected by consensus, spoils were distributed equitably, and judgments were fair. These ideals became solidified in traditions and in Islamic law. Could this vision of history be the link between two developments almost entirely unique to Islam: a millennium of military slavery and the terrorism of today?

CONQUESTS BY THE EARLY CALIPHS AND THEIR "JUST RULE"

There is evidence of a "just rule" in which the first four caliphs managed distribution of booty and payment of stipends to soldiers and to military retirees in an equitable way, this with one exception when booty and tribute had declined. Selected by consensus, they were called the "Rightly Directed Caliphs." Traditions have been accepted that give great honor to them. "The fiscal rectitude of the first four caliphs is given in profusion of detail," says one scholar writing of these traditions.[111]

When the early Muslim tribes vanquished the defenders of Palestine, Syria, Iraq, Egypt, and Iran, riches formerly unimaginable flowed to them. This booty and tribute was distributed by the caliph and by tribal chiefs to soldiers and others and included large numbers of prisoners. Some of the prisoners were ransomed, some of the women became wives, but most were enslaved as the property of officers and soldiers. With these riches, commerce in slaves and in many goods interested some of the tribal chiefs and officers, who profited additionally from this business. In the presence of great abundance, distribution might well have seemed fair, and this era of peace, glory, and just distribution of wealth has been imprinted on Islamic memory.

General satisfaction, however, did not last when spoils of war periodically contracted or had to be divided among larger numbers

111. CRONE, op. cit., 7.

of troops and retirees. Distribution of wealth and privileges became more difficult, and dissatisfaction among the soldiers periodically broke out in civil war. The first civil war brought the first ruling dynasty to power. Two decades later there were too many soldiers and retirees for the spoils, and despite the tax on non-Muslims, this stress led to a second civil war. The war made little difference, simply transferring power to a different branch of the first dynasty. The third civil war came about during hard times following the end of *jihad* in France and when the poll tax on non-Muslims was declining due to conversions. This third civil war brought a new dynasty to power, the Abbasid.

Thus, there is ample evidence that economic forces have been powerful in motivating Muslims since earliest times. Whenever the holy wars, *jihads*, yielded plentiful booty, many Muslims were willing fighters. Then, when few, or no, rich cities and fields lay ahead to plunder, interest in military service declined. To fill out army ranks, commanders first turned to captured men who had been freed after conversion to Islam. These men then voluntarily become "unfree-clients." Such soldiers made possible the occupation of Spain and an unsuccessful venture into France that ended in the year 737.

The military strength of the Abbasids, coming to power in 750, rested in eastern Iran and enabled expansion of the Empire into Central Asia and excursions into India and China. Both of the latter excursions met with defeat. The day when *jihad* was rewarded with rich booty was over. At the same time, an energetic army with a landed base in eastern Iran was fading away because Islam's inheritance provisions shrank farms into small plots and in time turned the owners into peasants. These changes combined with another factor in the precipitous decline in military service and loyalty to the caliphs: Pious Muslims did not relate to the worldly Abassid leaders and their administrators.

LONGING FOR THE SUCCESSES OF AN IDEALIZED PAST, ARABS TURNED AWAY FROM FLAWED LEADERS, WHO THEN RELIED ON MILITARY SLAVERY

Coolness to government was religiously inspired. During the 60 years after the death of Muhammad in the year 632, the Qur'an was assembled out of multiple fragments held by numerous individuals. In the two centuries or so that followed, the traditions about Muhammad and other early leaders were gathered, analyzed, rejected or accepted, and organized into books by self-appointed experts. During this era, religious legal scholars were formulating *shari'a*, Islamic law. This law was based on the Qur'an, on traditions, and on existing Arab-Muslim customs. Many of these customs were derived in part from a nomadic tribal past, but were also oriented to city life, rather than to the countryside and to farming, which Arab-Muslims generally disdained.

Much of this work in formulating the *shari'a* was done in Iraq. Patricia Crone explains:

> By 750 Islam had acquired its classical shape as an all-embracing holy law characterized by a profound hostility to settled states. The *Shariah* was created by men who had exchanged a [nomadic] tribal past for a commercial present in the cities of Iraq, outside imperial Iran and in opposition to the existing caliph.

> The *'ulama* [clerics] defined God's law as *haqq al-'arab*, the law of the Arabs . . . the consensus being that where God had not explicitly modified tribal law, he had endorsed it . . . The simple state of the Prophet and the first two caliphs in Medina was held up as the ideal while God's community was envisaged as an egalitarian one unencumbered by profane and religious structures of power below the caliph, who was himself assigned the duty of minimal government.[112]

112. Ibid., 63.

Guided by traditional and *shari'a*-directed visions, vainly hoping for a continuation of their tribal past, but then comparing all that to their actual lives, Muslims withdrew their interest in and support for government. This happened early in Muslim history. Daniel Pipes explains:

> As a result of the unattainable nature of Islamic public ideals, Muslim subjects in pre-modern times relinquished their political and military power. The populace stayed aloof from the decision makers. The clerics did their best to avoid serving as judges; some Sufis* refused to touch funds coming from an *amir* [tribal chief or king] on the grounds that they represented illicit gains. . . [Reputations of Muslims who did serve the government suffered.] All agreed that Muslim subjects should not become involved in public affairs.[113]

To summarize: Within a few decades of the death of Muhammad, leaders of prayers and other conveyors of the Prophet's messages sprang up from among the population, as did students of the Qur'an and collectors of traditions. Collectively these men became known as the *'ulama*. When men of religion judged that rulers, particularly the Abbasids, were lacking in virtue and not ruling justly, these religious figures gave voice to their opinions in the mosques, thus carrying pious Muslims along in this view and turning people away from government. A potent combination brewed: The pervasive spread of an attitude of withdrawal from public life and of animosity toward governments and leaders combined with the decreasing availability of war booty. As a result, men lost interest in serving in the army. There were no self-reliant landowners to come together and form an army.

The rulers had to hire troops from beyond the frontiers to protect their interests. The rulers eventually resorted to the use of military slaves. In this system boys or youth were captured, educated, and

---

* Sufism is a strand of Islam that is mystically oriented.
113. Ibid., 71.

trained for several years in the military arts to serve in crucial regiments in the royal armies. This methodical training of slaves for military service had been instituted by 840, and it continued to be used by various governments in Muslim areas for a thousand years.

Under the rule of the Ottoman Turks, military slavery was further developed. Slave soldiers were not needed at first when the Ottomans ventured out of their homeland into the Balkans, enthusiastically and vigorously fighting a new *jihad*, this time in Europe. Their "holy war" (which had nothing to do with the Crusades, then fading away in the Middle East) was hard fought, sometimes interrupted or set back, as it made advances for over 300 years. Beginning in the fourteenth century, Ottoman armies invaded Greece and Serbia, where they found abundant booty and were drawn further into Europe. Another war was conducted against a Shi'ite empire centered in Iran. Next they brought the Fertile Crescent, Egypt, and all of North Africa, except Morocco, into the Empire.

When invasion and plunder was giving way to occupation, the Turks became less interested in military service. Therefore, a new method of raising armies was developed. This method was based not on land ownership, but on control of land through the tax system, the *timar* system. A member of the elite was given a share in the agricultural taxes of a region, perhaps comprising several villages, in return for raising, equipping, and leading units of cavalry. At the height of the system, a *timar* leader could put over 100 horsemen on the field. At the same time the Ottomans enslaved boys from the Balkans. Those boys with special aptitudes were educated in the palace school to become administrators. Others were given strenuous military training and organized into special battalions of foot soldiers. All these slaves were owned by the sultans.

The abstract on the following page shows where and when military slavery was most predominant.

A Millennium of Military Slavery—From 850 C.E.

IN THE EAST

661–750. Umayyad Caliphate. (Ruled the Muslim empire.) In recurring periods, when the income from conquest declined, the Umayyads relied on unfree clients for military service. These clients had been slaves, were converted to Islam and given freedom, then voluntarily became clients for life.

850–932 and in the 1200s. Abbasid Caliphate. (Enjoyed respect in the Muslim empire from 750 to 1258.) Beginning around 820, the Abbasid rulers developed formal military slavery. Slave soldiers dominated the army after 850. When the Abbasids briefly revived in the thirteenth century, slaves again played a major military role.

932–1062. Buyids. The Buyids, a tribal army recruited as soldiers by Abbasid rulers, seized control in Baghdad. They quickly recruited Turkish slave soldiers.

c. 1062–1186. Seljuk Turks. (A power from 1038-1186; replaced Buyids in 1062.) The Seljuks, leaders of tribes of steppe warriors, made abundant use of military slaves in Iran. Near the time of the Seljuks' demise, slaves had almost taken control of this dynasty.

c. 980–1171. Fatimid Caliphate. (Ruled 909 to 1171 in Tunis and Egypt.) After taking Egypt in 969, the Fatimids quickly depended on Turk, Berber, Black, and Slavic military slaves.

c. 1200–1250. Ayyubids. (Ruled 1171 to c. 1250, replaced the Fatimids in Egypt.) The Ayyubids, free Kurdish and Turkish troops who had been successful under Saladin against European Crusaders, came to depend on slaves from Central Asia. Their military slaves—the Mamluks—usurped the throne.

1250–1517. Mamluks. (Slaves who ruled Egypt until 1517; influence lasted to 1790s.) Almost all Mamluk soldiers began their careers as slaves. When the Mamluks took control in Egypt, they passed their rule to other slaves recruited mostly from central Asia. They maintained a self-perpetuating slave oligarchy, even after the Ottoman conquest. They were driven out of Egypt in the early nineteenth century.

c. 1350–1826. Ottoman Sultanate. (In existence 1281 to 1924.) The Ottomans used military slaves from sometime in the fourteenth century to 1826. Slaves supplied the army with foot soldiers, the formidable Janissaries. Educated slaves played major roles in administration, including architecture.

c.1550–1732. A dynasty in Iran. This dynasty, lasting from 1501 to 1732, was brought to power by tribal troops from eastern Iran, then counterbalanced by slave soldiers.

IN THE WEST

c. 850–1031. Cordoba Caliphate. (Ruled 756 to 1031 by Umayyads.) First centered in Cordoba, then in Seville, this Caliphate enjoyed continuing support among the population, yet developed a slave system in the early ninth century. Slaves played a large role in the life of the dynasty.

c. 1125–1269. Two dynasties in North Africa. (In existence 1056 to 1269.) Both began as Muslim religious movements, but gradually came to rely moderately on slaves in their armies.

1228–1574. A dynasty in Tunis. Slave solders had a minor role.

c. 1530–1800s. Kingdom of Morocco. (In existence 1511 to present.) Almost from the beginning the kingdom depended heavily on Black African slaves, especially in the eighteenth century.

IN INDIA

Mughal Empire used military slaves erratically.

Sultanate in Delhi used military slaves.

Source: http://ww.danielpipes.org/article/448

Military slavery developed because ordinary Muslims viewed the early rule of Islam as entirely just, and, seeing flaws in later governments, were not willing to serve in their armies.

TODAY, TERRORISTS IDEALIZE THE EARLY YEARS OF ISLAM AND PLAN TO BRING BACK A TIME THAT NEVER WAS

Under the Ottomans the personal behavior of the people was governed by *shari'a*, and adherence to it in commercial and family matters played a critical role in the failure of their empire to keep pace with European progress and prosperity. In the eighteenth century, when European trade goods and some knowledge of Western customs entered into the Ottoman realm, the Wahhabi group, a rigid fundamental sect, formed in reaction.

Others were willing to learn from the West. In the nineteenth century, Western methods brought economic improvement for a portion of the Muslim population, and perhaps brought hope to many. Through the 1800s, European colonial powers continued to make significant inroads into the Ottoman Empire, and the influence of Western civilization grew, especially around the Mediterranean. Consequently, the influence of *shari'a* declined, and it was not reinstated when countries first gained independence in the mid-twentieth century.

However, there was widespread disappointment among Muslims when the influence of European commercial methods, the introduction of Western industries, the assimilation of modern military methods, the development of nationalism, the adoption of socialism, and the education of some Muslims in modern science all failed to improve living conditions for ordinary Muslim people. (Unfortunately, basic customs of the West—documented property ownership, the rule of law, and an end to bureaucratic obstruction of new businesses—were not introduced concurrently.) Some Muslims believed their economic plight and political weakness were due to their failure to resurrect the "just rule" of the first age of Islam, a rule they equated with *shari'a*. This was followed in the late twentieth century by the spread of existing Wahhabi ideas and the formation of other fundamentalist Islamic groups that would fight for the strict enforcement of *shari'a*.

Today's Islamic terrorists believe that they are reaching back to a time when the unified community of devout Muslims—the *umma*—fought holy wars to spread Islamic government across wide expanses of the known world. Of this unified community Daniel

Pipes writes, "The actual course of Islamicate history compares sadly with the ideal of a unified *umma* under a caliph waging *jihad* against non-Muslims only. . . . Indeed, Muslims fought one another far more often than they did the infidels; true *jihad* constituted a pitifully small percentage of their total warfare."[114]

Pipes points out that after the death of Muhammad, the unity of the *umma* under a caliph lasted only around 25 years, and ended when Muslims fought each other in the First Civil War. The community came together once again and embarked on more conquests until the Second Civil War. Then in 756 the *umma* was dramatically split when the Muslim ruler of Spain refused to recognize the caliph in Baghdad, and, "from that time on for about a century, a new regime became independent every five years," thereby pulling provinces away from the center in Baghdad.[115] The Muslim empire fragmented, and from around 950 and during most of the remainder of its existence the caliphate was headed by figureheads.

The *umma's* division into two factions became dramatic in the Early Modern Era, when relations between the empires of the Ottomans and the Iranians, one Sunni, one Shi'ite, became intolerant and, on the part of the Ottomans, aggressive and murderous. Fighting among Muslims had occurred throughout history, but the extent of this bloody fighting was unprecedented in Islam and ignores the Qur'an, which says that Muslims must not kill Muslims.

The public ideals of Islam have remained unattainable. Yet Muslims prefer the vision of their glorious first community. "Regardless of divisions and warfare among Muslim kingdoms, the community of Islam did not lose its allure. . . .The *umma*, or community, is permanent, grand, universal."[116]

114. DANIEL PIPES, op. cit., 67.
115. Ibid., 66.
116. Ibid., 67–69.

The history of Islam shows that *shari'a* was never thoroughly applied. As experience was gained through the centuries, Muslims made adjustments despite their respect for shari'a. Pipes says:

> In public affairs, Muslims did not live up to most Islamic precepts and ideals: the rates of taxation prescribed by Islam for *zakat* were unworkable in an agrarian-based economy and were displaced already in the 9th century; the [Islamic] juridical procedures were too inflexible for use in a system of justice; commercial restrictions, such as the prohibition on interest, were absolutely untenable for traders; and the political-military requirements were beyond the reach of any mundane government. No people has ever lived long by these laws of Islam—over a millennium of history makes this point clear beyond dispute. . . . It is my assumption that Muslims in pre-modern times did take these ideals to heart and therefore the failure to enforce them had major consequences. Muslims shared a disappointment in the conduct of public affairs: illegal taxes, non-Islamic judicial tribunes, usury, and failed political-military institutions. [117]

These words "no people has ever lived long by these laws" were written in 1981 just as—in some countries—the laws were being tried anew. In that year, the Iranian ayatollahs were clamping their religious law of Shi'a down on their people, and in the two and a half decades since then they have severely damaged the economy and drastically increased the poverty of their people. The Iranian example of repression has spread to Syria. In Iraq, the presence of a large Shi'ite population seemed overwhelming, and the response was the oppressive rule of Saddam. In Libya, Qadhafi ruined his country's economy. Algeria has been "saved" from religious repression by a harsh military regime. Saudi Arabia continues to impoverish its people by adhering to the severe Hanbali form of Islamic law favored by the Wahhabi.

An unavoidable conclusion confronts us: People can survive and increase their population under Islamic law and Islamic charity, but

117. Ibid., xvii.

only with the destruction of generalized prosperity and stunted development of the people.

Today's terrorists are attempting to recreate the characteristics they believe prevailed during the "Glorious Days" of early Islam. They equate this with *shari'a*. In their retrospective view, the early Arab army was imbued with religious fervor and completely united by inspiration from Allah and the Prophet and his immediate successors. They see the ancient *jihadists* living by the words of the Qur'an (fragments remembered but the whole not yet assembled), by the traditions (not yet gathered and selected), and by Islamic law (in a period before its legal scholars were born).

EPILOGUE

THE REFORMATION OF ISLAM

Bernard Lewis concludes his book, *Crisis in Islam*, with an extremely serious warning:

> If the leaders of Al-Qa'ida can persuade the world of Islam to accept their views and their leadership, then a long and bitter struggle lies ahead and not only for America and Europe. . . . Sooner or later, Al-Qa'ida and related groups will clash with the other neighbors of Islam—Russia, China, India—who may prove less squeamish than the Americans in using their power against Muslims and their sanctities. If the fundamentalists are correct in their calculations and succeed in their war, then a dark future awaits the world, especially the part of it that embraces Islam.[118]

Tawfik Hamid, a Muslim scholar and writer, locates the fault in the spread of Salafism, or Salifi Islam, an ultra-conservative version of the religion. He writes, "It is vital to grasp that traditional and even mainstream Islamic teaching accepts and promotes violence."[119] His examples are the killing of those who leave Islam, disciplining women by beating, justifying war against non-Muslims to subjugate them, and exhorting good Muslims to exterminate Jews before the end of the world. In recent decades the world has seen 150,000 people killed in Algeria, hundreds of Buddhists killed by Muslims in Thailand, and today the massacre of Sunnis and Shi'ite of each other in Iraq. Hamid says violent Muslims are encouraged by well-meaning people in the West who restrict themselves to criticism of the West and, under the umbrella of cultural relativism, extend kindly understanding to those who commit atrocities.

Hamid was once a member of a fundamentalist group, but began to preach peace. For this he was driven out of his homeland, Egypt, and today does not disclose his location. He says there is a

---

118. LEWIS, op. cit., 154.
119. TAWKIF HAMID, "The Trouble with Islam," *Wall Street Journal*, 4/3/2007. Hamid is also the author of the book *The Roots of Jihad, An Insider's View of Islamic Violence*, 2006.

lack of theologically rigorous interpretations approved by scholars that clearly challenge the abusive aspects of Islamic law, shari'a, and he has been developing interpretations of the Qur'an and traditions that promote peace.

DISSUADING TERRORISTS FROM VIOLENCE

Sayid Imam Al-Sharif founded the Egyptian *jihad* organization that was responsible for the assassination of President Anwar Sadat and the killing of 62 tourists from the early 1980s to the mid-1990s. After 9/11 he was imprisoned in Egypt. In these facilities prisoners have been allowed to consult with each other and have dialogues with clerics from the University of al-Azhar, the fount of mainstream jurisprudence for Sunni Muslims. During this experience, Sayid moderated his views and wrote the book, *Advice Regarding the Conduct of Jihadist Action in Egypt and the World.* Other top ideologues of the *jihadists*, now mostly freed, have written 25 volumes of revisions called *Corrections of Concepts.*

A diplomat commented that these reappraisals have "kept violence at bay but their views are still pretty sinister." They retain the goal of spreading the rule of Islamic law throughout Islam and beyond. [120]

Indonesia employs former terrorists who have sworn off most types of violence to go into the jails and prisons, working to convince would-be terrorists that attacking civilians is not acceptable to Islam and that it alienates average people from their religion. Along with vigorous police action, this course of "deradicalization" has been effective. Similar programs have been developed in Saudi Arabia, Jordan, Yemen, Singapore, Malaysia, and even Pakistan.[121]

---

120. Joshua Kurlantzick, *Salt Lake Tribune* (Special to the *L.A. Times*), 1/08/2008.
121. Jan Black, *The Guardian*, 7/2/2007.

Deeper Changes Are Needed for Prosperity

Peace, of course, is a necessary condition for prosperity. Further changes or reforms are needed to bring lasting prosperity to Muslim lands. Goals of re-creating the seventh and eighth centuries (for Sunni Muslims) or the eighth and ninth centuries (for Shi'ite Muslims) must be abandoned. In those centuries, the economic system was agrarian, despite shining examples of handicrafts and commerce. Ancient laws and traditions when applied today starve and crowd out connections among humans and opportunities that are necessary for economic security in the twentieth and twenty-first centuries.

A key characteristic of the Islamic law is the strong male dominance, in which male honor is tied to how completely a man controls the women in his family and in which a woman rates half the value of a man in a legal context. She seldom is allowed to deal independently with the outside world. The status of women is "the canary in the mine" in terms of predicting how well the broad-based economy will perform in Muslim lands. This "canary" tells how strictly the *shari'a* is administered, and how fond the people are of ancient traditions. Among those old laws and traditions are provisions that prevent a wife who well understands her husband's business or farm from effectively aiding her husband, and, after his death, from perpetuating that enterprise. Likewise these laws and customs make it difficult for any family member to maintain the enterprise and impossible for a third generation to do so. Wealth, therefore, gravitates to government and to the clerical class, all too often supporting tyranny.

Whenever Islamic fundamentalists are able to take power, their rule will severely hamper the creation and preservation of new productive property by ordinary people. With power in their hands and vigorous preaching of their brand of Islam, they will be able to control people's lives. Existing tyrannical rulers will be replaced with another form of tyranny. Ayatollah Mirza Hussein Ma'ini saw this around 1900. He said:

> Among the forces safeguarding despotism are the religious tyrants. They adopt certain words and components to appear appealing to the naive. . . .They claim to safeguard the religion and to be looking after the interests of the religion, but in fact they spread the shadow of Satan over the public and keep them under this ominous shadow of ignorance and wretchedness.[122]

Under the rule of *shari'a*, unemployment will continue to be high, and—despite Islamic charity—most people will be struggling. All the while, ruling elites will retain wealth and power by a combination of government oppression, favoritism, generous subsidies for food and power, and heaping blame on the West for their plight. While there is some truth in the claims of Western responsibility for serious problems in the Middle East, such a focus blocks the best avenues to overcome problems. It prevents self-examination and cuts off learning from the successes of other countries around the world.

The pious Muslim prays five times a day, and among the prayer's statements is this: "Welcome good fortune." While not exactly a request for good fortune, if good fortune comes through the will of Allah, then it will be accepted with pleasure. It is ironic that standing in the way of good fortune is religion's chokehold on many aspects of Muslim life that distort and cripple the economy.

Some Muslim governments are taking steps toward economic reform. For example, King Abdulla II of Jordan noted in January 2004 that "the Arab Business Council has issued a blueprint for economic liberalization, good governance, and human development," and a number of Arab countries endorsed a declaration on democracy and human rights. The king also noted that Jordan has raised its standards for education, has a well prepared work force,

122. M. MOHADDESSIN'S *Islamic Fundamentalism*, 176.

and has an elected parliament, but, he points out, "elections are only part of democratic life: stable systems of civic rights and laws are essential." His government has backed out of direct control of the media and is opening the airwaves to private television and radio. A legal review seeks to ensure that laws do not discriminate against women. Islam has a proud tradition of humanistic values, declared the king: "Equal dignity of all people; respect for reason and law; tolerance and personal responsibility," adding further that "these values will drive a new era of progress in the Middle East." Despite these factors, the king warns that "for reform to succeed, the Palestinian-Israeli conflict must be solved." [123]

The need for improvement of the basic economic structure comes to the forefront occasionally among Muslim scholars. Muhammad Siddiqi, an economist, wrote that a "major cause of poverty and need, in which about half the population of Muslim countries finds itself, is the inequitable distribution of land and other income-yielding assets." This, he says, can be remedied with land reform, grants of stock with some small payment from the recipients, and help in setting up small businesses. [124]

He does not explain how such distributed assets can remain the property of ordinary Muslims when subject to inheritance laws. One must recognize that the time of Muhammad was profoundly different from the present. Did the Prophet really intend for endless division of productive property? When the Prophet was in Madina, often conducting war, there was not much in the way of productive business assets brought into existence by individuals through years of work. Long-distance trade had suffered a decline, and these businesses were no longer dominant. He was dealing with windfalls of booty, excess wealth easy to divide up. It is logical to assume that the purpose behind his statements about heirs was his

123. King Abdullah II, "Reform Is Our Priority," Wall Street Journal, 4/16/2004.
124. M. N. Siddiqi, The Role of the State in the Economy, An Islamic Perspective, 1996, 147.

desire for everyone to benefit, sadly made impossible over the long term by the same statements.

Say that a man has two camels and little else, and he has 4 sons and 6 daughters, but no wife. The sons are to receive twice as much as the daughters. (4 boys × 2 shares = 8 shares for the boys. 8 shares for the boys + 6 shares for 6 girls = 14 total shares.) Certainly Muhammad would not want the camels sliced up. Would he expect that their milk, hair, earnings from cartage, and their offspring for as long as the two camels live be divided into 14 parts so that each of the four sons can receive two parts of the production and each daughter one part? For such a small part in the reward, what son or sons would take care of the camels and put them to work? What daughters would be able to? If colts are born, then who owns them and who would do the hard and dangerous work of training them? When the illustration is applied to a farm, say in early Madina, the same awkward problems occur. Who is going to find it rewarding, or even possible, to work a small plot of land? Muslims need to find a way to exempt from their onerous customs of inheritance the kinds of productive property that call for close attention by an interested and capable owner. They must find a way for pools of wealth to grow outside of the government and the religious foundations.

ISLAM, A RELIGION OF WAR OR OF PEACE?

Why do terrorists attack Western countries, Western tourists, and Western officials who are abroad? First of all, to Muslims the union of religion and state is the only situation possible. With that background, the world is divided into *Dar al-Islam* and *Dar al-Harb*. In *Dar al-Islam*, Muslim authorities are in charge and their laws prevail. *Dar al-Harb* is territory controlled by non-Muslims where non-Islamic laws are applied. This is considered land of the enemy. In the Islamic view, the two are in an unending state of conflict. This becomes a source of "anti-other" diatribes and can easily trigger a state of war. This ancient view was first sketched during the time when early Arabs were conquering all before them, and military action was profitable. Today, however, military action is economically destructive to both the victors and the vanquished.

In addition, a recent idea has provided a rationale to fight those considered to be infidels. A doctrine recently appeared among Islamic fundamentalist writers in which Quranic sayings that were spoken later in the Prophet's life outweigh his earlier declarations. Thus, Muhammad-ibn Ahmad ibn Juzayy al Kalbi, a fundamentalist scholar of modern times, wrote, "The order to be at peace with the infidels, came before the order to fight them. . . . All of these references are abrogated by verses of the Qur'an 9:5 and 2:216. And you are prescribed to fight." He is quoted in a widely circulated pamphlet, *The Neglected Duty*, which was written in an Egyptian jail in the 1960s by Muhammad 'Abd al-Salam Faraj to arouse "all Muslims in despair." Faraj also quoted scholars who claimed that the Verse of the Sword (9:5) annuls all treaties and defense pacts made with infidels. *

"Islam's Silent Majority"

An opinion piece with the above title appeared in the *Wall Street Journal* in 2002. The piece brings rays of hope. The author is Robert Asghar, a Los Angeles-based editor of management and leadership books and the son of a Pakistani immigrant.

He looks at a school he visited as a teenager where innocents have recently been killed. In his home town of Karachi, the *Wall Street Journal* reporter, Daniel Pearl, lost his life, and in Islamabad,

*Note: The Historical Background in this book briefly discusses the assembly of fragments of the Qur'an during a period of rapid conquest and civil wars. Verses to embolden soldiers were placed early in the book. A young man inclined to violence would not come across thoughts of peace until he was much further along.

near where he once lived, a church was attacked. He has been asked, "Is Islam a religion of peace?"

To combat the culture of hatred pushed by the Pakistani *madrasas*, religious schools, his father used a significant amount of his life savings to build new schools in his hometown village in order to offer a liberal education and economic opportunity to marginalized youths. "People like my father will need the support and protection of like-minded moderates." But he complains that too many Muslims are more concerned with competing forms of religion than by "the demonic forces rumbling in their own camp. Too many hundreds of millions of Muslims can tolerate, rationalize and even promote violence. All this must change, and change now." [125]

Ashgar replies to his questioner:

> Granted, the language of the Koran can seem aggressive and belligerent to some ears. But let the graceful image of Prophet Mohammed, depicted by scholars such as Huston Smith, become the normative one for Muslims and Westerners alike. The prophet was long-suffering and merciful toward Meccan authorities who had abused him during his ministry. Let a Palestinian child meditate on that. Let Muslims tolerate no lower standard of civic life, and divorce all those who would object. . . .The five million Muslims who call the United States home are the best candidates to step forward and set this standard. Doing so would give Islam an authentic claim as a religion of peace. [126]

AN IMPORTANT ROLE FOR AMERICAN MUSLIMS

Feisal Abdul Rauf is the *imam* of an important mosque just twelve blocks from the World Trade Center in New York City. He reminds us that the three Abrahamic religions, Judaism, Christianity, and Islam, share the two greatest commandments: to love God with heart,

125. Robert Asghar, "Islam's Silent Majority," Wall Street Journal, 8/9/2002.
126. Ibid., Editorial page.

mind, soul, and strength and to love our neighbors regardless of who they are just as we love ourselves. "Whenever each religious tradition has honored these commandments, it has contributed to humanity's growth and progress. Whenever one has failed, it has contributed to conflict and disease both within its own society and between its society and that of others."[127]

His example of success is the Cordoba Caliphate in Spain where, in a climate of tolerance and pluralism, a high and prosperous civilization appeared. From that history Imam Rauf fashioned the Cordoba Initiative, which makes use of education and dialogue among Jewish, Christian, Muslim, and secular organizations "to help repair the damage that has been done to Muslim-American relations over the last fifty years."[128] He appeals to American Muslims for leadership because they are aware that it is "a country whose systems remarkably embody the principles that Islamic law requires of a government."[129]

Rauf urges the formation of a "peace team" made up of Islamic and Western legal scholars, religious leaders from many world religions, economists and banking experts, conflict resolution experts, educators, communications experts, psychologists, and social scientists. He stresses that these people must be deployed as a team all at once in order to move the work along rapidly. The issues are urgent. Essential to the process are American Muslims who understand the cultures of both East and West.

He also hopes that the United States government will assist Muslim nations to attain four major objectives. Some of the high points are given below:

1. Establishing the basic economic infrastructure: "the creation or reform of banking systems, capital and stock markets, and

---

127. FEISAL ABDUL RAUF, *What's Right with Islam*, 2004, 2.
128. Ibid., 275.
129. Ibid., 80.

sound monetary policies." These policies can help bring freedom from poverty.

2. Establishing the rule of law, including an independent judiciary.

3. Promoting broader public participation in government and promoting protections of human rights. He says this does not mean overnight conversion to full democracy, an impossible and "not altogether meaningful" task.

4. Fostering an Islamically articulated separation-of-powers that would mean an independent judiciary, a free economy with safeguards against monopoly and corruption, a military that does not interfere in governance, a free press, and freedom of religious expression and protection of religious institutions. [130]

Imam Rauf calls attention to the Islamic way of considering all interest, no matter how low, as usury and therefore forbidden. He notes the consequence, the impossibility for Muslim countries to control the currency, controls that are exercised in other countries through banking and interest rates. Inflation tends to get out of control, quickly wiping out savings and causing suffering among the people. (In an earlier chapter I included prohibition of interest as a serious problem, but it did not originally occur to me that this renders a government unable to control the value of its currency. Without this ability, its citizens are left to twist in the winds of inflation.)

From my point of view, I wish Imam Rauf had also recognized the role played by ownership of productive property. Ordinary Muslims must be encouraged to create productive assets and be allowed to bequeath these assets as they deem beneficial to their families and to the enterprise over the long term.

Perhaps a "breakthrough" could be made if Muhammad were seen as a leader deeply concerned for the economic well-being of all

130. Ibid., 252–255.

his followers, not just for his elite advisors. This is obvious when one looks at the broad moves of his life from an economic point of view, rather than trying to reconstruct his daily life as a way to derive burdensome, detailed laws that might have been suited to the first century of Muslim existence but today are destructive anachronisms.

REINTERPRETING ISLAM IN THE LIGHT OF MODERN KNOWLEDGE

A remarkable book on Islam was written a half-century ago by a number of Islamic academicians and two diplomats. Muhammad Rasjidi expresses himself in the chapter on "Unity and Diversity in Islam." At that time he was the Ambassador to Pakistan from the Republic of Indonesia.

> While it might be true that those who lived in the time of the Prophet could understand religion better than the people of today who must study Islam by means of documents only, we cannot ignore the considerable change in social situation and world conditions in the past fourteen centuries. The insistence on imitating the predecessors reflects a loss of self-confidence which was at one time widespread in Islamic communities. The texts of the Qur'an are still and always will be valid, but we should understand them in the light of present knowledge. One of the great tasks facing religious scholars in our time is the re-examination of the jurisprudence of Islam in the light of reason and modern knowledge. Since Islam does not make a distinction between the secular and the religious, and since a large part of the Muslim world has but recently attained political independence and is not playing a significant role in world affairs, this re-examination of Islamic law is all the more urgently needed.[131]

Historian Albert Hourani writes, "Islam is what was deepest in them [the Muslims]. If to live in the modern world demands

131. Morgan, editor, op. cit.

175

changes in their ways of organizing society, they must try to make them while remaining true to themselves; and this would be possible only if Islam was interpreted to make it compatible with survival, strength and progress in the world." The historian quotes the Egyptian Muhammad 'Abduh (1839–97), whose writings have had a lasting influence. "In his [Abduh's] work a distinction emerges between the essential doctrines and its social teachings and laws. The doctrines are belief in God, in revelation through a line of prophets ending in Muhammad, in moral responsibility and judgement—and they can be articulated and defended by reason. Law and social morality, on the other hand, are applications to particular circumstances of certain general principles . . . When circumstances change they too should change."